Maurice Daly

Daly's Billiard Book

MAURICE DALY

Edited by William Welton Harris

Diagrams and Maps by Frederic P. Mitchell
Photographs by Albert Hedley

Dover Publications, Inc.
New York

Published in Canada by General Publishing
Company, Ltd., 30 Lesmill Road, Don Mills, Toronto,
Ontario.
Published in the United Kingdom by Constable
and Company, Ltd.

This Dover edition, first published in 1971, is an
unabridged and unaltered republication of the
second edition, as published by A. C. McClurg and
Company in 1914.

International Standard Book Number: 0-486-25724-X
Library of Congress Catalog Card Number: 73-142874

Manufactured in the United States of America
Dover Publications, Inc., 31 East 2nd Street, Mineola, N.Y. 11501

DEDICATION

THIS volume is devoted to the extension among amateurs of a better understanding of the theory and practice of "position play" in "ball-to-ball" billiards. In particular, it aims to make clearer and of practical value the methods of modern experts in "system" play. It considers shots in their serial relation rather than as individual strokes, and lays stress not so much on the shot to GET the balls together as the shots to KEEP them together.

It is dedicated to the amateur billiard players of America; and should it attain, even in small degree, the objects intended, it will be sufficient recompense for the years of study and work involved in its preparation.

MAURICE DALY

CONTENTS

PART I

PART II

CONTENTS

PART I
By the Editor

Daly's Billiard Book

CHAPTER I

PURPOSE OF THIS BOOK, WITH SOME INTERESTING
FACTS CONCERNING THE DEVELOPMENT OF POSI-
TION PLAY TO ITS MODERN FORM, AND THE
SHARE TAKEN THEREIN BY FAMOUS PLAYERS

ONE who really desires to excel in any department of
human endeavor must, unless he be of that quality
of genius which is a guide unto itself, seek out in print
those things which other men have learned, and thus
easily and quickly add them to his own equipment. In
this lies the greatest value of printing.

In astronomical study, for instance, one takes his
basic mathematics as developed in turn by Assyrian,
Arab, Greek, Roman, monks of the Middle Ages, and
all the others down to the present-day expositor of the
mysteries of the calculus and of the fourth dimension.

Book Study of Games.— In games, too, the wise man
takes advantage of the experience of others. The whist
student reads Hoyle, Elwell, or Foster. The golfer
studies Vardon, Taylor, Braid, or Travers, besides taking
lessons from his club professional.

Strangely enough, in light of these admitted facts,
each billiard player who would learn the really modern
game is forced to traverse almost the whole ground anew.

Position Play Neglected by Writers.— The writer has

1

had the pleasure of examining such books on the technique of the game as are obtainable and some that are rare and out of print — this both in English and French. Only one —"Modern Billiards," an excellent work and well worth while — is at all easy to find. It is issued by the Brunswick-Balke-Collender Company.

And while giving these writers credit for their painstaking efforts, it was the fact that in not one of all of these books is the matter of position play in its *modern* niceties entered into, except as to the *first shot*, that caused the writer to attempt the task of presenting in print that single thing that every billiard player most needs — a helpful presentation of "position play." That is the one thing that makes the game a never-ending study and joy.

"Sequential-ness" of Shots.— There is in no other available work any suggestion that certain broad *principles* of play may be developed to guide the player to a solution of his position play problems; no suggestion of arranging shots in general categories; no indication of — and perhaps nothing is of more importance — what tempting shot to *avoid* — tempting by reason of the certainty of the immediate count of one point, treacherously deceptive because it adds to that certainty the probability of no more. In other words, the "*sequential-ness*" is not the thing emphasized, but the count, in nearly every diagram in all billiard books up to this time.

"Second Ball Play" (*"Landing" Right*).— Of "second ball play"—that refinement of position work that marks one of the greatest differentials between the

old game and strictly modern billiards — of that not a word. Cushion shots? Yes! "Ball to ball" system play, nothing!

Given an average player, one who can play simple caroms, understands the "draw" and "follow" shots, can average, say, around one (that is, can make 100 points in 100 innings at straight three-ball billiards) — where in printed form can he find any explanation of the baffling fact that he, who can execute single shots as well as the man who can average five or more, and who runs sometimes from twenty-five to fifty, cannot make these contrary ivory balls behave for him. It is this want that circumstances, almost by accident, led Mr. Daly and the editor of this volume to try to fill.

Needs of the Average Player. — It is the point of view of the average player that is in this volume regarded as of the greatest importance and which has been constantly kept in mind.

In this manual the major attention is given not, the reader will notice, to description of fancy shots, nor, except in a small degree, to directions for the acquirement of that delicacy or extremely fine calculation which the highest class professional must undertake, but to the production of an easily understood guide to the acquirement of the billiard knowledge which, from a good, ordinary "leave" (the kind that every player is constantly getting), will enable this average player to roll up runs of at least 5, or 6, or 8, or 10 points, instead of 2 or 3.

MAURICE DALY, THE TEACHER

Let us hope it will not be too personal to tell about

the chain of circumstances and the deciding reason that led to the writing of this book.

It so happened one winter that the editor of this volume put in an afternoon playing billiards with Maurice Daly in his New York academy. Mr. Daly could not help, though he said never a word while playing, but teach. He teaches for love of the game, and many of our best amateurs, yes, and professionals, owe to him much of their equipment and skill. The teaching instinct is in him.

Even as Frank Ives came to be known as "The Napoleon" of billiards, as Jacob Schaefer "The Wizard," George Slosson "The Student," Maurice Daly should be known as "The Teacher." And who shall say that this old winner of three world championships, who still has the famous "diamond cue," although less than "The Napoleon," "The Wizard," or "The Student" in fame as maestro, has not the greater gift?

And as an example of his progressive ideas let me remark in passing that it was Mr. Daly who first suggested and put in practice in a tournament in 1913 the rule of separating "frozen" balls by a card. He is ever experimenting.

Added to the afternoon with Mr. Daly, above mentioned, others followed, and then more. Those winter afternoons began with the pupil just the ordinary player found anywhere, to whom a run of fifteen was a rare delight. In comparatively few weeks averages of better than five at eighteen-inch balk-line, and runs of better than thirty were frequent, and occasionally the fifty-mark was passed. One happy day he averaged sixteen in two hundred points. A "straight-rail" run of one hundred and ninety-two and a balk-line run of seventy-four still later lent cheer to the heart and an exhilaration that is still not dead. Blessed by these happenings of kind Fortune the writer determined that others should share such of his instruction as he could make clear by diagram and printed word.

Now let it be said that the credit for this manual is Mr. Daly's. Every word of its technical text on "position play" proper has passed under his exceedingly strict blue pencil. Many of the diagrams he personally drew. All were personally suggested, and personally supervised, and many redrawn several times to meet his strict demands. All are taken from the storehouses of his billiard information. The writer had the advantage and pleasure of cooperation in the work, doing, as it were, the secretarial labor and attending to the many details necessary to publication in both newspaper and book form. The three maps alone are solely of the editor's invention, but they came from Mr. Daly's explicitly stated views, so the credit for them is his.

Sources of Information.— The editor must assume responsibility for the introductory chapter and for the chapter on preliminary work for the beginner in billiards. They are founded upon a playing experience of more than twenty-five years, a personal and billiard playing acquaintance with or careful observation of the methods of such masters as Maurice Daly, Frank Ives, Jacob Schaefer, George Slosson, George Sutton, Ora Morningstar, Albert Taylor, José Ortiz, Calvin Demarest, Louis Cure of France, Thomas J. Gallagher,

Albert Cutler, Leonard Howison, Eugene Carter, Harry Cline, Koji Yamada of Japan, Timothy Flynn, and Alfred de Oro among the professionals, and of J. Ferdinand Poggenburg, Edward W. Gardner, Martin Mullen, Wilson P. Foss, Orville Oddie, Jr., Charles F. Conklin, Morris D. Brown, Lucien M. Rerolle of France, Edouard Roudil of France, and Albert Poensgen of Germany, besides numerous lesser lights.

It so happens that with the exception of — at this date, 1913 — George F. Slosson and Thomas J. Gallagher, Maurice Daly is the only prominent player living in America whose span of playing years is coincident with the complete development of the modern game of carom billiards. His professional career has put him as opponent to practically every master of the cue in all the years from the sixties, beginning with Michael Phelan, down to the present day. And while his active competitive career closed with the decade of the nineties, before the days of Willie Hoppe, George Sutton, and Ora Morningstar, yet he helped develop their play, and has had the opportunity of studying their style, system, and methods to the most intimate detail.

With Mr. Daly to watch was to study, to compare, to analyze, to assimilate, and to make of value to other students.

Maurice Daly was born in New York City, April 25, 1849. His mother's cousin, Dudley Kavanagh, the first American professional champion, had several billiard rooms in the city, and thus it was that at the age of thirteen he began his billiard career. Yet, while leaving school thus early, young Daly never ceased being a student. He has traveled extensively in Europe and elsewhere, and has widely read, and in his trips abroad with other players his knowledge of French has often served the entire party.

Early Billiards and Players.—Beginning himself to play publicly in the later sixties, he has had the opportunity to study the play of all the experts in that formative period of the game. In those days billiards was generally played on the big 6 by 12 or $5\frac{1}{2}$ by 11 pocket table, with four balls. It was not until the seventies that the pure carom game, on a 5 by 10 table, became standard and the number of balls reduced to three. In those days the "rail nurse," the "balk line nurse," etc., were unknown. The massé shot had just appeared. It came from France, and Mr. Daly's recollection is that M. Bergér first showed it here as a standard shot.

Michael Phelan, sometimes called "the father of billiards," a fine player who flourished in the forties, fifties, and sixties, and who got the starting capital for his billiard table manufacturing career by winning a $15,-000 match in 1859 from John Seereiter, wrote a book on billiards, which is curious and interesting at the present day. Of the massé shot he said: "None but an expert will attempt this shot. The cue is held very upright, and care must be taken not to let the cue tip touch the cloth or a tear will result." Good advice it is still.

Appearance of the Three-Ball Game.—The three-ball carom game, while not becoming standard until the seventies, began to be played to some extent by the experts in the later sixties, but still on the 6 by 12 pocket table. How enormous one looks to us now!

Position play, as we know it, was unknown to even the best of them.

It is curious, indeed, to note the scores in "class" games. In 1863, only two months after Dudley Kavanagh had become champion, he played a match with Isidore Gayraud for $100 a side, and beat him 150 to 141, averaging 1.49/100, with a high run of 11. Funny, isn't it? Mr. Daly was marker in that game. In 1868, A. P. Rudolphé, in a match with John Deery (both afterwards champions), won with 150 to 100, averaging 5, and 30 was his high run. And that was top-notch billiards at that time. And it must be remembered that the multiple system of counting prevailed, caroms counting two or more, according to the balls struck, and pocketing the balls also counted in multiples.

First Championship Tournament.—The first tournament in America at the three-ball game for the championship of the world was held in New York in 1873, and Maurice Daly tied for first place with Albert Garniér and Cyrille Dion, the Canadian. Garniér, the Frenchman, won the play-off. Knowledge of the game had progressed so that the winner ran 113 in this tournament and one player got up to an average of 17.11/17. It was in this year that George Slosson and Jacob Schaefer had the first of their almost countless matches. Slosson won with an average of 5.5/11, but Schaefer had the high run of 45. No balk lines then, remember.

I speak of these records merely to show the particular stage of the development of systematic position play that marked the billiards of that time. Young Daly was there to see it to note the various position plays as they were developed, to see the game grow. As he in later years rose to a capacity of averages as high as 50, and runs in the hundreds at the 18-inch balk-line game (he averaged 40 at 18.1 with the writer, at 400 points, only recently), it shows the long route over which he had to travel.

Some of this increase in speed is due undoubtedly to the improvement in tables, tools, cushions, cloth, chalk. Cues in those days were generally long and light; today they are shorter, stockier, and much heavier. And last, but not least, is the improvement in table lighting.

The old-day players will tell you that in the skill of making the single shot the early players were the equal of anyone today. Jacob Schaefer could, for the single shot, do almost anything in the seventies that he could do in the nineties. But where he was wanting was in the knowledge of how to "flock the ivory sheep." He lacked knowledge, not skill.

Many a player today knows more billiards than he can execute. In fact, nearly every good amateur knows the theory of the "rail" and "balk-line" nurses. Only a few can make them heavily remunerative. Nearly every professional knows the theory of the "anchor." Only Ives and Schaefer ever had the marvelous mastery of nerves and muscles to make big runs by it.

Let us look at a list of the names of the masters who developed the game, and all of whose methods Daly knew and studied intimately. I name holders of championships only, with the date of their first winning that honor. I bring the list up only to the time of Frank Ives, for the reason that with the exception of George

Sutton's improvements in the balk-line nurse no later players have developed anything that ranks as an important discovery of system in play.

Beginning in the later sixties, with Michael Phelan, he has studied the billiards of the following champions: Dudley Kavanagh (June 9, 1863, to May 16, 1865), Louis Fox (1865), John Deery (1865 and 1866), Joseph Dion (1866 and 1867), John McDevitt (1867), A. P. Rudolphé (1870), Frank Parker (1871), Cyrille Dion (1871-1873), Albert Garniér (1873), Maurice Vignaux (1875), William Sexton (1877), Jacob Schaefer (1879), George F. Slosson (1880), Frank C. Ives (1892).

Each of these had his personal excellencies, his idiosyncrasies, and each has contributed to the fund of billiard information which has led to the game as it is today. In Daly's billiard "college" the faculty has included every famous professor of the last forty years.

In the sixties the game began to be too fast as played by the experts and an era of limitations set in. First the two side pockets were dispensed with. Then all the pockets. In the early seventies the three-ball game supplanted the four-ball game as the professional test.

Birth of the "Rail-Nurse."—Authorities differ as to the exact details of the birth of the "rail-nurse." John A. Thatcher, in "Billiards Old and New," holds that a nurse played by Rudolphé may be considered the germ of the idea. Maurice Daly rather gives the credit to a nurse played by Joseph Dion. Rudolphé, with the balls "frozen" close together on the rail, as shown in Plate No. 1, would often make quite a run, say, from a dozen points to twenty, before breaking them. Dion's plan of operation was different in that he started with one ball out from the rail a bit, similar to the "anchor," as we know it. He would cross the face of the balls with a carom, and on coming back for another carom would work the balls back to or near the original position. This is also shown on Plate No. 1.

Sexton and the " Rail-Nurse."— But it must be noted that both these plans contemplated holding the balls in one place or near it. It was a *stationary nurse*, not a "*running*" nurse. William Sexton, ac-

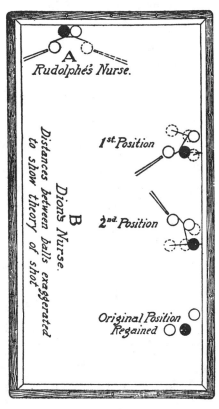

PLATE 1

cording to Mr. Daly (others say Jacob Schaefer, though the probability is that both men worked it out about the same time), got the idea of carrying the balls along the rail as a running nurse, and in their hands it reached its perfection. The "rail" was speedily mastered by other experts until runs into the hundreds, and even the thousands, became matters of record. Maurice Daly was the first to cross the 200-mark in an important competition, and got a warm kiss from an enthusiastic French professional for the feat.

The balk-line nurse, too, is a running nurse; indeed, it is an adaptation of the rail nurse, played at longer range from the cushion. The "anchor" and "chuck" nurses are stationary nurses. A running nurse leads from a given position through a series of steps to a renewal of that original position, and so on ad infinitum.

But fully as important development of the time was the mastery that these early players attained in *getting* the rail from various positions. Sexton, Schaefer, Daly, or Harvey McKenna would get the rail position in a few shots just so surely as they got the balls at the end of the table. They would get the rail where the ordinary player would not see the chance. And as the man who got it first was almost sure to pile up a big run, they practiced *getting* the rail by hours from countless positions in the end of the table, just as later Ives practiced getting the "anchor" position, or as nowadays experts practice getting the line.

A fuller exposition of some of these devices will be found in Part III under chapters devoted especially to advanced play.

Marvelous Runs on the Rail.— On May 15, 1879, Jacob Schaefer, in a championship match with George Slosson, ran out the 1,000 points in three innings (5, 690, 305), an average of 333⅓. On April 10, 1880, in Paris, Maurice Vignaux made an 80 average in a 4,000-point match with George Slosson, and made a run of 1,531. Slosson made a run of 1,103. Such work put straight-rail billiards to sleep as a competitive test for professionals.

It may be noted in passing that in 1887, at Boston, Harvey J. McKenna made an average of $416\frac{2}{3}$ in 5,000 points, and ran 2,572 and 2,121. In San Francisco, May 29, 30 and 31, 1890, Jacob Schaefer ran 3,000 points, unbroken. So it came about that schemes had to be devised to handicap the skillful players.

The Day of Cushion Caroms.—All through the late seventies, and well into the eighties, the favorite plan was to confine the play to cushion caroms, and a grand game it was. Unfortunately it is too little played today. Never a better game, Mr. Daly holds, for the development of billiard skill! It was at cushion caroms that Maurice Daly and William Sexton attained world pre-eminence and their greatest fame. They were regarded in the later seventies and early eighties much as Schaefer and Slosson were in the late eighties, Schaefer and Ives in the nineties, Morningstar, Sutton, and Hoppe in the first decade of the twentieth century. They were the "king pins" of the billiard world.

The "Champion's Game."—It was in the 1874 three-ball tournament, won by Maurice Vignaux, that a "balk" line first appeared. It was a line drawn diagonally across the corners from points on the side rails $5\frac{1}{2}$ inches from the corner. This was to prevent "crotching" the balls in the corner and to stop the progress of a rail-nurse. Afterwards the triangular space was increased by making the beginning points of the balk-line further down the side, generally 14 inches on the end rail and 28 on the side rail, as shown in Plate No. 2. This was termed the "champion's game," and it was at this game that George F. Slosson first won a championship.

Its riddles were easy to masters of the rail-nurse. It had short vogue. Schaefer quickly showed how to nurse the balls along the rail to the contact point of the balk-line and, "turning" the balls, nurse them back again. Or he would "turn the corner" and start down the side

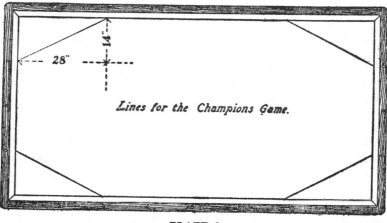

28"

14

Lines for the Champions Game.

PLATE 2

rail. The champion's game as a vehicle for public competition began in 1879 and closed in 1884.

Appearance of True Balk-Line.— Many plans for balk-lines have been suggested and some tried, but all have been discarded for the plan familiar at the present day. The lines are now drawn parallel to the side and end rails, 18 inches from the cushion. At first 8-inch lines were tried, then 12, then 14, and now 18 is the standard. It was over 14-inch lines that Ives did practically all his greatest playing in competitions, although he made records at 18-inch. The 18-inch line became standard after his premature death from consumption in Mexico.

In the balk-line game, with lines drawn on the cloth as shown in Plate No. 3, there are eight rectangular spaces around the table near the rail and a mid-table space. In the middle the player may make all the points he can without being called upon to drive a ball outside the "balk space," as it is called. But he must in the 18.1 game ("one shot in"), whenever both object balls are within any one of the balk spaces along the rails, drive at least one of the object balls across a line on the very first shot. It may go out and come back, but it must at any rate go out.

In the 18.2 game ("two shots in") he must drive at least one of the object balls across a line not later than the second shot after the object balls are "in balk."

Mr. Thatcher, in "Billiards Old and New," credits Benjamin Garno, a noted writer on old-time billiards, with the suggestion of the continuous line around the whole table, terming it a "balk"-line. Heiser suggested that the lines intersect and the balk-line, as we know it, had its first public tournament in 1883 at 8 inches. Vignaux's average of 44 5/6 in 3,000 points the following year caused the lines to be set out to the 12-inch position, and this was tried briefly in 1885. The 14-inch line became popular that year, and the extension to the 18-inch position was not found necessary, by reason of added skill of the players, till the nineties.

In 1893 the full possibilities of the "anchor" were first realized and demonstrated by Jacob Schaefer, even as he had been a pioneer with the rail. Great, indeed, he was, and many hold him to have been the greatest player of all, master of the best of today.

It is to be noted here that Frank C. Ives invented no standard nurse. They had been discovered when he appeared. But he mastered them all. To him billiards was distinctly an intellectual problem; to Schaefer the game was a vehicle for the manifestations of inspired genius.

The runs at the "anchor" by these two, the only

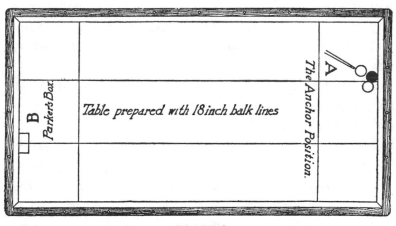

PLATE 3

players who ever really mastered it, brought the "box" at the contact points of the balk-lines to limit it. Charles Parker, of Chicago, suggested it, and "Parker's box" with the anchor position are shown in Plate No. 3. The same plate shows also the 18-inch balk-lines.

The secret of the "anchor" play is to kiss softly from the first ball, just "grazing the glisten" of the second ball without moving it from its place, then playing back to the original position, just grazing the first ball and kissing up from the second ball, leaving it still against the cushion. This process is then repeated.

Runs at the Anchor Nurse.— Schaefer ran 343 at the anchor against Ives in a match in November, 1893, in New York, and Ives answered Schaefer the following night with 456 at the same anchor nurse. In December, also in New York, Schaefer scored 566 at the anchor against Ives.

In January, 1894, Ives, in a tournament, had a run of 487. Parker's box followed. Yet there is no reason why amateurs should not practice the anchor.

Today the standard test for amateurs is 18-inch balk-line, the balls to be put out of balk not later than the second shot (18.2), and the supreme professional test is the 18.1 game.

Benefit of Rail-Nurse Practice.— In this treatise Mr. Daly explains by word and diagram (something which has never before been done in print) the rail-nurse in all its details. The rail-nurse is the *foundation* nurse, its principles applying in *every other form of close manipulation.* It should be studied for the benefit of the general game, for upon its mastery skill at all the other nurses is founded. No practice for the billiardist is more conducive to the development of delicacy of touch, sub-conscious appreciation of force, and of the amount and kind of "English" required in all close manipulation. No other practice will so certainly restore the stroke lost through excessive three-cushion carom play. It is of the highest value as manual training for other ball-to-ball billiards.

The accomplished violinist practices "bowing" by the

hour. The pianist works on his "scales," other hours on "fingering." And so the billiard player, to acquire mastery of his game, should pay attention to the fundamentals.

In this work Frank Ives stood supreme. If, as some-one has said, "Genius is the capacity for hard work," then Ives had genius. He would spend from four to six hours a day on the "anchor," for instance, or the "chuck," trying in various ways to *get* these conventional positions from various leaves. Other hours he spent on single-cushion shots or on massés, or on close manipulation to "go through" the balls.

In 1893, before his celebrated match with John Roberts, of London, one of the really great billiard players of the world, Ives spent an average of four hours a day practicing on a big English game table (6 by 12) with the small balls, perfecting the anchor and the rail-nurses with these tools. It was his great run of 2,540 in a position near one of the corner pockets similar to the anchor-nurse that enabled him to defeat the great Roberts at the English game, and win thousands of dollars for himself and many friends. He made the run at the anchor, but he had to use the rail-nurse to get the balls to the place where they became anchored.

Roberts and the Rail-Nurse.——Roberts was to England what Maurice Vignaux was to France, what Schaefer and Ives were to America. But he did not know the rail-nurse. Afterward, when under Ives' instruction he mastered it, he doubled and trebled his previous records.

In patient practice Ives outdid even Slosson, "The

Student." No other great player spent such time over the details, unless perhaps we except the work of George Sutton on the "line"-nurse, at which in his best day he led all the rest.

CHAPTER II

SOME PRIMARY POINTS FOR BEGINNERS

HALF the battle, if not more than half, is in beginning well. A player will have twice the chance of developing a really good game of billiards if at first he acquires a good style.

And what is good style? I use the term to indicate the position at table and a method of stroke which leads to mechanical accuracy and ease. There may be grace as well, but that is in large part a question of the physical attributes of the player. It would be difficult, indeed, for Albert Poensgen, the great German amateur, to acquire grace with his six feet two inches of height, his long legs and arms, and short body. No amount of practice could ever make his attitude and stroke look like that of Jacob Schaefer. Yet his stroke is one of the most accurate.

How Masters Differ in Stroke.—Great artists differ. Jacob Schaefer, Willie Hoppe, and Maurice Daly were not blessed with height. They learned billiards in boyhood, when even shorter than in later years. Naturally they learned to hold the cue off to one side and rather high. They could reach the balls in no other way.

Maurice Vignaux, George Slosson, Martin Mullen, Calvin Demarest, Thomas J. Gallagher, Alfred de Oro, and Edouard Roudil stand for ordinary shots more directly over the cue, the forearm hanging down and swinging like a pendulum from the elbow as an almost motionless pivot. This is the style that gives least of the "side-to-side" or "teetering" (up and down) motion in swinging the cue back and forth. For all except short men this is the style which beginners will do well to acquire.

Even as the violinist practices bowing, the pianist fingering, and the golfer the "swing," so should the beginner learn a good style of stroke at the very start. Then no bad habits are formed which it is almost impossible thereafter to break.

If this style be orthodox, it is true that Schaefer, Daly, and Hoppe have become great artists with unorthodox styles. It is a question, however, if their methods of stroke have not, nevertheless, been an impediment rather than a help.

The importance of a good style is urged, not because it is a *sine qua non* of success but because it is of very important assistance. Personally, the writer of this chapter is of the opinion that these men have become great players in spite of their cueing style.

Calvin Demarest, under the tutelage of his early-day teacher, Lansing Perkins, and later by himself, has carried this study of cueing style further perhaps than any other prominent player of the day, and the hints hereafter following are along the lines he follows in instruction for beginners.

Style for Older Players.— To players of long standing with methods already "set," I would say: "Do not attempt to change unless you are prepared to learn bil-

liards all over again, and to practice the new style for at
least three afternoons a week for a month before again
playing a contest game." You may not think that
worth the trouble, though the writer did, and experienced
a most pronounced benefit in his game as a result.

The Cue.— No professional or amateur of note today
uses a cue lighter than 20 ounces, and 22 ounces is the
weight used by most players. Willie Hoppe uses 20 and
21-ounce cues. Frank Ives used a 23-ounce cue, and
Miss May Kaarlus, the fancy shot player, used a 24-
ounce cue.

The Tip. — Use only the best French tips. Let them
be not too small, medium in hardness, and of fair thick-
ness. Better too thick than too thin.

The Grip.— It is important to cultivate a good, firm
grip that will give a smooth, yet " solid," stroke and
command of the delivery of the tip to the cue ball. Do
not take the cue too far forward. (See Plate 4.)

The very loosely held cue has a special use more particularly in making long or quickly acting draw shots,
but for ordinary work it is better to err on the side of
holding the cue too firmly, rather than too lightly.
Better in the full hand than in the tips of thumb and
finger only. (See Plate 5.)

Do not take hold at the butt end. This will give a
" teetering stroke " ; that is, the up-and-down motion.
(See Plate 6.)

The Right Way to Grip a Cue.— Let the cue sink
solidly into the curve between the first finger and the
thumb, the major part of the " squeeze " of the hand
being done by the roots of the thumb and base of the

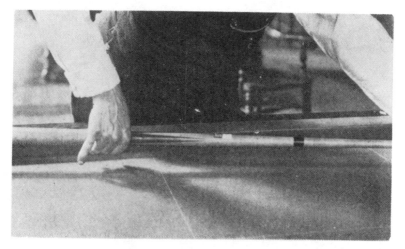

PLATE 4

Showing "grip" too far forward

PLATE 5

A poor "grip," in the finger tips

PLATE 6

Another poor grip—too near the butt

PLATE 7

The best place to grip the cue

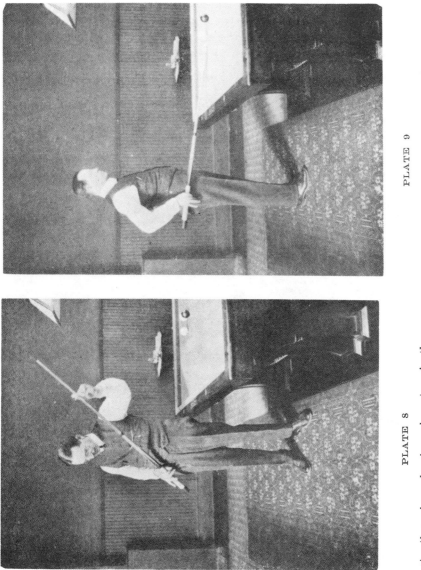

PLATE 8

Another view, showing where to grip the cue

PLATE 9

Rest hand on hip bone, over trousers' seam

PLATE 10

Face directly forward, heels together

PLATE 11

Tip of cue over center of cue ball, giving proper
distance to stand for ordinary shot

forefinger. Take hold of the cue just a shade forward of or at the center of the twine whipping on the butt. This is the point where the cue balances the best. This grip gives not only solidity, but permits the full measure of wrist flexibility. (See Plate 7.)

Light and Loose Grips.— For quickly acting *short* draws some players seize the cue solidly, almost with a squeeze, with a whole fist grip. They say it forces the cue " through the ball " better, makes a fast draw, with less force going into the object ball. For a *long,* quick draw the very loose grip seems to be more effective.

To Get a Good " Stance."— And now let me point out a sure way of getting a good " stance " (position), to draft a very expressive golfing term, for any ordinary shot, be it draw, follow, or " spread " (wide-angled carom), or " dead ball."

Now, do this slowly, one step at a time, and do it over and over again. It may seem artificial at first, but, like the violinist's artificially acquired method of bowing or the golfer's painfully practiced " swing," it becomes second nature. In time you will do it instantly and absolutely unconsciously. You could hardly do it otherwise.

Step 1.— Take the cue solidly in the U formed by the thumb and forefinger, gripping the cue just a shade forward of the center of the whipping on the butt. (See Plate 8.)

Step 2.— Rest the big thumb joint of the cue hand on the point of the hip bone, over the seam of the trousers. (See Plate 9.)

Step 3.— Face directly forward, along a line parallel

to the line the cue ball is going to go on the shot. Don't face the cue ball itself. Heels fairly close together. (See Plate 10.)

Step 4.—Let the tip of the cue (the hand still resting on the hip) just reach to the top of the cue ball, without any sensation of leaning forward to reach that point. Your distance, now, from the cue ball is exactly right for all ordinary shots in the open table. (See Plate 11.)

Note at this point: you are now facing squarely forward, directly in the line of play. The cue points a straight line from the hip along a course the ball is to follow. But note this particularly: you are not facing the cue ball. But you will feel in your arms and body the aim of the shot, just the feel the pitcher has in his muscles when about to pitch the baseball, or that the archer has when about to let go with his arrow, or the boy about to throw a stone. They do not sight with the eye, as the marksman does; they feel it all in the muscles.

Step 5.— Advance the left foot (or right foot for a left-handed player) a *moderate* step, *directly* forward. Not too long a step, not too short, and don't straddle or sprawl. (See Plate 12.)

Step 6.— Now turn the *toe* of the *right* foot a little outward. Don't turn the HEEL inward, but the TOE outward. (Left foot for a left-handed player.) (See Plate 13.)

Step 7.— Place the bridge hand solidly and *well spread out* on the table for your bridge. Next arch the hand, and then rest the cue on the V between the thumb and first finger, as shown in detail on Plate 19.

Step 8.— Settle back! That is, as it were, "sit

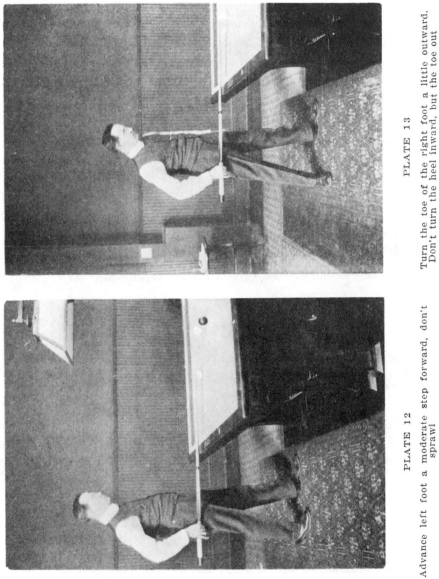

PLATE 12

Advance left foot a moderate step forward, don't sprawl

PLATE 13

Turn, the toe of the right foot a little outward. Don't turn the heel inward, but the toe out

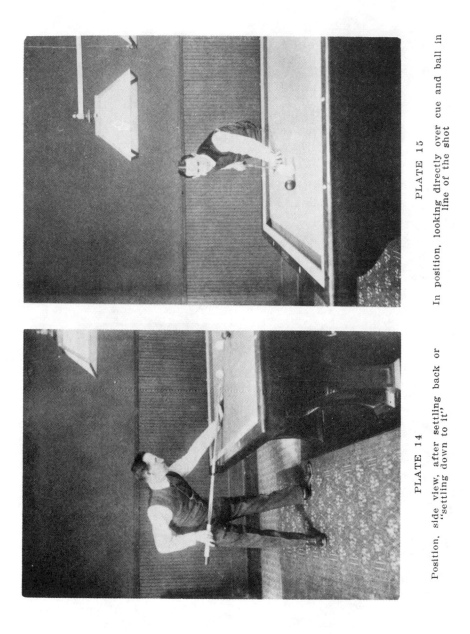

PLATE 15

In position, looking directly over cue and ball in line of the shot

PLATE 14

Position, side view, after settling back or "settling down to it"

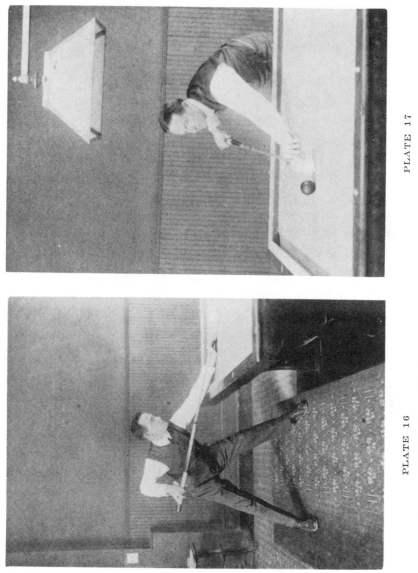

PLATE 16

A common but bad stance, side view

PLATE 17

Front view of common but bad stance

down " a bit to the shot. You are now in a perfect cue position. (See Plate 14.)

Your eyes are now *directly over the line of the cue and the ball.* You are looking straight ahead through *both* eyes, not out of the corner of the eyes or sidewise. (See Plate 15.)

In Plates 16 and 17 you see common but extremely faulty positions, where a good sight at things is much more difficult.

In the position advocated the natural pendulum swing of the forearm, hanging from the elbow, the *upper* arm moving little, if any, gives a cue swing freer from side strains than is possible from any other position. In this position there is no tendency toward rocking, teetering, or jerking. In this position, having once got set for the stroke, *you may shut your eyes* and still make the finest hairline shot across the table.

Like the pendulum, which always swings in the same arc, your swinging cue arm swings where it ought to, because there is nothing to pull it aside.

Left-Hand Shots Made Easy.— And it will almost at once give you the power, invaluable in good billiards, of making left-hand shots almost as easily as right. You can even make left-handed massés, if they are not too difficult.

I do not declare that this plan is one without which you cannot succeed. I put it forward as of the highest value for learners, and for established players if they care to devote the time necessary to unlearning old but less efficacious methods and to acquire the " feel " and incidental mastery of the new. This will take some weeks, perhaps, but the steps above will give anyone a perfect position at the table.

Power in a Good Position.— Great power of stroke is possible to nearly any player with this stance and stroke. Nine cushions can be struck, a feat few players can perform.

A sixteen-year-old caddie boy with a good swing can drive a golf ball further than the strongest man with a bad swing. All his power is applied in direct lines, and no muscular energy is lost. Little Miss Kaarlus, the fancy shot player, now retired, could make shots hardly possible to any other player. Yet she was a mere slip of a girl in her teens, weighing, say, 120 pounds. It is not *muscle;* it is properly directed force.

Control of Force.— With this position a higher degree of control of force is readily attainable. The power of the stroke is to a greater degree than in other styles controlled by the length of the swing rather than by the force of the punch.

The Bridge.— But now to another important point, the bridge. A " solid " bridge is of very great importance. I advise the use of two styles of bridge, one for " dead ball " shots and follows and caroms without " English," the other for draws. But I do not advise this to the exclusion of the one-style bridge so much used by most good players. The usual bridge is the locked-finger bridge. (See A in Plate 18.)

It is used in all styles of shots. The slight faults with it are these: that for shots where the cue tip hits the ball at center or above the hand naturally " curls up " some to make the bridge higher, and thereby be-

A. THE ORDINARY LOCKED FINGER BRIDGE.

B. AN IMPROVED LOCKED FINGER BRIDGE. FOR DRAW SHOTS ONLY.

PLATE 18

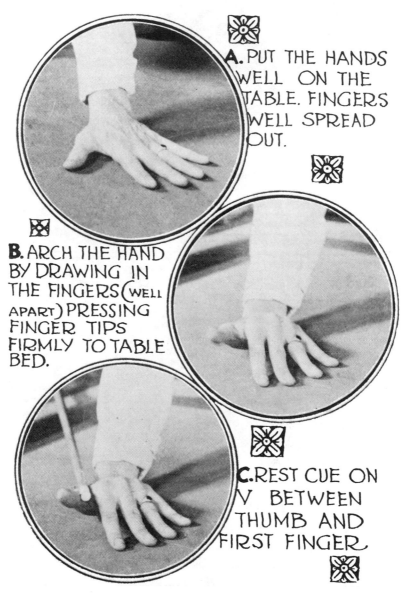

A. PUT THE HANDS WELL ON THE TABLE. FINGERS WELL SPREAD OUT.

B. ARCH THE HAND BY DRAWING IN THE FINGERS (WELL APART) PRESSING FINGER TIPS FIRMLY TO TABLE BED.

C. REST CUE ON V BETWEEN THUMB AND FIRST FINGER

PLATE 19

comes less solidly founded on the table. The bridge hand rocks more easily.

For draw shots it does not easily get low enough. Therefore, I advise a slight modification of the ordinary locked-finger bridge for draw shots, by simply tucking the long middle finger under the palm. It will surprise you to see what a help this is. (See B in Plate 18.)

This bridge is used when the tip hits the ball below center. The open-hand bridge is used for " dead ball," follow and carom shots when the tip strikes center or above center. But it must be made right, and this is the way to do it. (See Plate 19, A, B, and C.)

Step 1.— Place the whole hand, wide open, finger well *spread apart*, flat on the table. Let the " heel " of the palm rest firmly. (See A in Plate 19.)

Step 2.— Now draw up the fingers, pressing the tips firmly against the cloth. Keep the fingers well spread apart. (See B in Plate 19.)

Step 3.— Let the thumb point slightly upward, making a V between the thumb and the base of the finger. Slide the cue in this V, which is so made that the roots of the thumb and forefinger can even squeeze the cue. (See C in Plate 19.)

The Stroke.— Now you are in position to let the forearm swing easily, like a pendulum, from the elbow. Let your cue hand keep firm hold of the cue. Do not cramp up the hand or curve the wrist. The fingers are pointing toward the floor, but just naturally curved a trifle around the cue. The cue motion will be partly in the wrist and partly in the forearm, just as the motion of a good penman is partly in the fingers and partly in the forearm.

The bridge hand is, say, eight to ten inches from the cue tip for ordinary shots, back stroke not too long.

The "Follow-Through."—When a good billiard stroke is made, it is, as Thomas J. Gallagher happily phrases it, a "measured" stroke. That is, it has no jerk. The cue "flows" smoothly forward. Though checked, of course, by the weight of the ball, nevertheless it *does not stop when the tip strikes the ball.* The tip seeks to go on *through* the ball, as a golfer would term it; that is, it goes on well beyond the point where the ball lay. (See Plate 20.) And while the cue is checked in speed, it is not by reason of the player intentionally slowing the stroke.

Le Coup Sec.—In passing, there is a short, sharp shock of a stroke that the French call "le coup sec" (dry stroke), which is useful in certain cases; for instance, when the cue ball is against a cushion and you wish to get a sharp, wide-angle carom shot. "Le coup sec" is a stroke with the least possible "follow-through."

Center-Ball Stroke to Get a "Dead Ball."—In a center-ball stroke (i. e., cue tip striking the ball in the center) the cue tip, when it passes the point where the ball lay, has a tendency to seek the cloth. For, as the cue comes forward, the cue butt comes up into the palm of the cue hand, which closes around the butt. (See Plate 21.)

The "follow-through," or the feeling that the cue is going to follow through, is the *sine qua non* of a good draw or follow shot. The good stroke is not (except in special cases) the hammer tap (le coup sec). In fact, if you have trouble in making draw shots you find help

PLATE 20

Showing how the tip in a good stroke "goes through" the ball

PLATE 21

Showing how in a "center ball" stroke for a "dead ball" the cue tip
seeks the cloth after "going through" the ball

in trying to make the tip of your cue push the cue ball against the object ball. You cannot possibly do it, but you will get the "follow-through" and a beautiful "draw" effect. It cannot help but draw if the tip strikes the cue ball below center, but not so far below as to cause a miscue.

Cause of Miscues.— In passing, it may be said that miscues come almost invariably from one of two things: striking the cue ball too low, or elevating the butt *just as the stroke is delivered,* in an effort to strike low

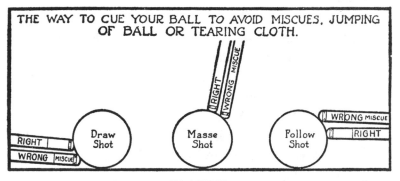

PLATE 22

at the last instant. A good draw shot can be made with a tip which has not even been chalked if the stroke is delivered properly. Ninety-nine times out of a hundred the tip was not to blame when you made a miscue; it was your faulty stroke. Most miscues come, either in massé, draw, or follow strokes, from striking the ball too near the edge. (See Plate 22.)

Strokes Crescendo and Diminuendo.— Now another important point. A good stroke must be made "crescendo," as the musicians say; that is, increasing in speed until contact. If the cue is traveling at an increasing rate (or, at any rate, not lessening) when the tip meets the cue ball, the effect will be obtained. If you "spare" the stroke, as the golfers put it, or flinch, or "let up" on it, the speed of the stroke becoming "diminuendo" (lessening in speed), the shot will fail in effectiveness. Many an intended wide carom, by reason of a flinching, diminuendo stroke, degenerates into a sickening follow. Timidity, for fear of driving the object ball too far, will cause you to "spare" the shot, with a resultant "foozle."

To Gain Accuracy in Draws and Follows.— An important point about draws and follows is accuracy, for often it is of the most vital importance to land on the second ball in a certain spot, or on the edge. *Too long a back swing tends to swerving of the cue,* with resultant inaccuracy. So do not overdo the back stroke. Better to err on the short side in making the back stroke than in bringing the cue too far back. And this is true also of follow shots.

Importance of Concentration.— The importance of mental concentration on the shot can hardly be overestimated. Mr. Daly, in a series of billiard articles in the "New York Herald," wrote as follows, and it is pertinent at this point of the discussion:

"First, make up your mind what shot you are going to attempt before 'addressing' the ball (taking cue position). Concentrate your attention on the spot of the *first object ball* which you are going to hit. Carefully avoid letting the eyes wander, while delivering the stroke, away from that spot to the carom ball. Half of the success in executing shots lies in the permanent habit of concentrated attention on the FIRST ball."

Avoid Fiddling.— I may add to this a caution against certain bad habits. Avoid waste motion and excessive preliminary fiddling.

Aim Where You Want to Hit.— Aim the tip of the cue at the spot of the cue ball you want to strike. Some players aim low and then shoot high or right or left. Some aim right and in making the stroke cross over and hit left, or *vice versa*. These bad habits result in uncertainty of the amount of English or follow or draw, in miscues, or in " no action " when English is needed.

CHAPTER III

DIAGRAMS FOR BEGINNERS

THE writer will take it for granted that the reader already knows the rudimentary shots at billiards — the plain carom, the follow, the draw, and the plain-angled

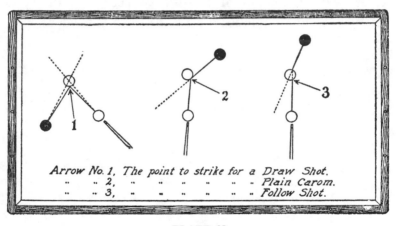

Arrow No. 1, The point to strike for a *Draw Shot*.
" " 2, " " " " " " *Plain Carom*.
" " 3, " " " " " " *Follow Shot*.

PLATE 23

cushion carom. But he will present here some phenomena — without any attempt at too exact and scientific an explanation — which have a direct bearing, not so much upon the single count, AS UPON POSITION PLAY possibilities.

Simple Angles.— In Plate 23 is shown the way to determine, usually, the point on the object ball to hit for a plain, simple carom, a simple draw, or simple **follow**.

These will serve as bases, and variations from these must be learned by experience.

For instance, note the spot indicated on the object ball in Plate No. 23, diagram No. 3, for a follow shot. That means hitting your cue ball above center. If you hit the same object ball in the same spot with your cue ball hit below center you get a draw shot.

Plain Caroms.— First let us take up the plain carom and note some of its peculiarities due to friction of the cue ball on the cloth on its course to the object ball, these points often having a great bearing on position-play possibilities.

In Plate 24 are shown three plain carom shots, stroke delivered at moderate speed. In diagram A the cue ball

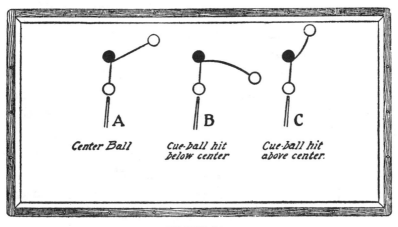

PLATE 24

is hit center and the cue ball travels from object ball to carom ball in practically a straight line.

In diagram B the cue ball is hit below center. The slight **backward** spin of the cue ball tends to draw the ball back in the direction of that backward spin, on account of friction with the cloth.

In diagram C the cue ball is hit above center. The

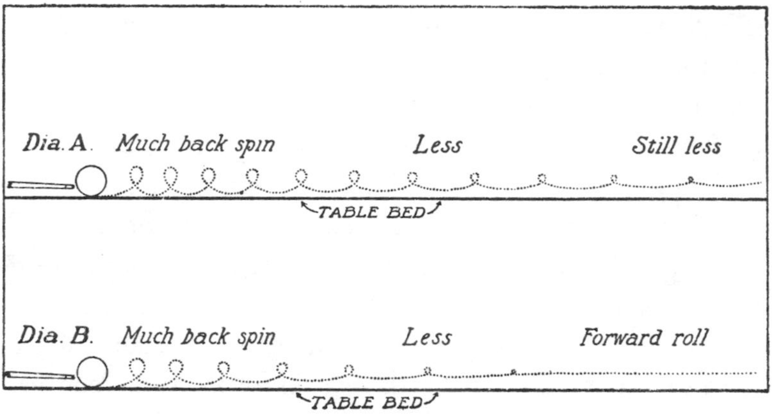

Dia. A. Much back spin   Less   Still less

TABLE BED

Dia. B. Much back spin   Less   Forward roll

TABLE BED

PLATE 25

slightly accentuated forward spin tends to curve the ball forward, from the same causes.

An increase of the speed of the stroke tends to accentuate the curves from the direct path. These facts are frequently of importance in choosing shots for position play.

The Effect of Drag.— In Plate No. 25 is shown a position in which the drag or showing effect of the draw stroke (below center) is illustrated. The player's object is to hit the two balls softly, so as not to scatter them. There never was a geometrically perfect ivory sphere (all have porous centers), nor a perfectly flat billiard table. A slow ball going the full length of the table will roll off the direct line. So, if the ball is hit harder with " drag " it keeps its line, slows down from the effect of the friction of the cloth, and lands softly. A slow follow made from a distance is shown in the same plate, diagram B. The effect of the drag is lost just before the object ball is hit, the cue ball has started rolling forward, and a follow shot results.

Angles of Incidence and Reflection Not Equal.— It will be seen that the angle of incidence against a billiard table cushion is not always equal to the angle of reflection. A ball cued on top tends to rebound at a wider angle. A ball cued on the bottom tends to a sharper angle. (See Plate 26.)

A ball hit hard sinks into the cushion and comes out at an angle more acute. With a lively cushion the phenomenon is even more marked. No two tables are exactly alike as to cushion speed, for rubber is a fickle

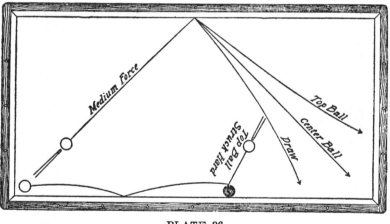

PLATE 26

thing. Then, too, a tight cloth is "faster" than a cloth under less tension.

Difference in Elasticity of Ivory.— Again, similar

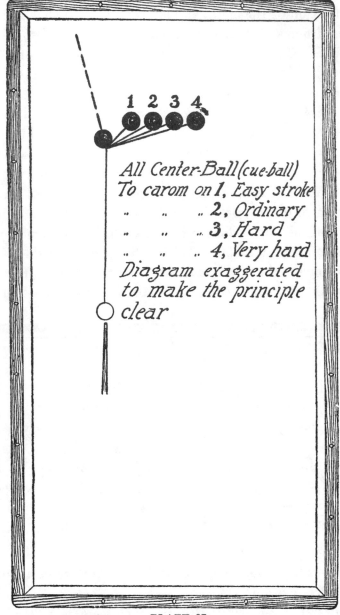

1 2 3 4

All Center-Ball (cue-ball)
To carom on 1, Easy stroke
" " " 2, Ordinary
" " " 3, Hard
" " " 4, Very hard
Diagram exaggerated
to make the principle
clear

PLATE 27

phenomena are observed with reference to varying ivory. An old, cracked ball is less resilient than a new ball. A cold ball is less resilient than a warm one. Rubber, too, is less resilient when chilled. Every ivory ball has a porous core, and the centers of gravity of no two balls are exactly alike. Balls expand and contract under changing temperature almost as readily as mercury. And they expand more in one dimension than another, due to the grain of the ivory.

This shows why it is futile to attempt to give diagrams with exact angles, notations of exact degrees of force, etc. We can show general principles only, and practice and experience must guide the player.

Now as to varying resiliency of ivory in its effect on carom shots. (See Plate 27.)

Ball on a Curved Course.—The pupil will also note that with a draw stroke, the cue ball (striking object ball in the center) comes back in a straight line. If the line back be not directly back, but off at an angle, the cue ball in coming back sometimes describes more or less of a curve. This is due to the fact that the contact between cue and object balls not being full center, the cue ball passes the spot where the object ball lay before the draw spin takes full effect. (See Plate 28.)

Plate 28 illustrates these tendencies toward increased curvature of path, increasing as to angle off a direct line back is increased.

Top English. — In general, remember that a cue ball struck above the center tends to swerve "forward" (in a line parallel to its course from the cue tip to object ball) after contact with either a ball or a cushion.

A cue ball struck below the center and *having a back spin at the time of* contact tends to swerve backward, and a curve (called the "swell") results after a contact with either a ball or a cushion.

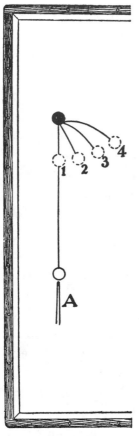

A ball struck into a cushion at speed, with top, bottom or side spin, tends to come out from the cushion more affected by the English than a ball struck softly. Only in the case of a ball struck very softly and without English is the angle of incidence equal to the angle of reflection.

Side English.—Now let us examine another very important phenomenon having a bearing at all times upon position play as well as on "the count." If a cue ball be struck by the cue tip to the right or left of its center (on the "side," if there can be said to be a side to a sphere), the ball will go not only forward, but it will also revolve at a greater or less speed around its up-and-down axis,

PLATE 28

to right or left, depending upon which "side" the ball was struck with the cue tip. When this spinning ball strikes a cushion and settles into it, the spin, by its friction in gripping the cushion cloth, tends to throw the ball, on its recoil, away from the natural angle.

This side spin is what we term "English," though in England they call it "side" or "twist." Now, here is the first thing about English for the beginner to bear in mind:

Right English throws the ball on the rebound to the right of the natural angle.

Left English throws the ball on the rebound to the left of the natural angle. (See Plate 29, diagram B, Nos. 1, 2, and 3.)

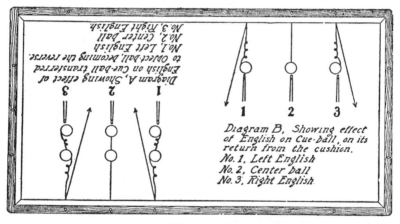

Diagram A, Showing effect of English on Cue-ball transferred to Object-ball, becoming the reverse.
No. 1, Left English
No. 2, Center ball
No. 3, Right English.

Diagram B, Showing effect of English on Cue-ball, on its return from the cushion.
No. 1, Left English
No. 2, Center ball
No. 3, Right English.

PLATE 29

English the ball on the side *toward which you want the ball to go.* We will point out later that the use of English is altogether too general by beginners, and that it should be used, as a rule, only when a special effect is sought, and not for the ordinary cushion shot.

Effect of English on the Object Ball.— Another effect must also be noted. The English on the cue ball tends to transfer itself to the object ball on contact.

When the two balls are placed in stationary contact

the point of contact is hardly more than a pinpoint in size. But when a ball at speed strikes another, both balls, being extremely elastic, flatten out some, and the point of contact is larger (Mr. C. C. Curtis, by experiment, has calculated that it is sometimes one-fourth of an inch), just for an instant. Golfers often notice the same thing after a full shot, the print of the golf ball on the face of the club is often as large as a twenty-five-cent piece.

Now, the spinning cue ball rubs on the object ball and tends to make it spin; but note! in *the opposite direction*. The amount of that transferred English, though slight, is quite often enough to affect the rebound of the object ball from the cushion to a degree very important in position play. This action is shown in diagram A (Nos. 1, 2, and 3) of Plate No. 29.*

Direct and Reverse English.—Right English on the cue ball when the latter is aimed at the right side of the object ball is called "natural," or "direct," English. But left English on the cue ball, the latter being aimed to hit the object ball on the right side, is called "reverse English."

In other words, "reverse" means English on the side

---

* Mr. C. C. Curtis, of New York, has made many interesting experiments with billiard balls, and contends that the spin of the cue ball is not to any appreciable degree transferred to an object ball, not enough to "throw" the object ball off a true angle from the cushion. The writer is convinced he is right, and that what really happens is that the cue ball takes a curved course to the object ball, striking it at a point off the one aimed at. But for practical purposes of billiards the student will get the effects he wants if he takes the idea of the Diagram A, in Plate No. 29, as actually true. They serve to show the point in practical use, and are simple to understand, and hence are used.—THE EDITOR.

opposite to the side on which the object ball is hit by the cue ball, be it right or left. (See Plate 30.)

"*Reverse*" *on the Cushion.* — When a ball with right English strikes a cushion to the right of the direct line it tends to throw the ball on the recoil still further — and *with added speed* — to the right. This is often of great importance in position play. Left English on the same shot is called "reverse" and tends *to slow* the ball after its recoil from the cushion and prevent it going so far to the right in its recoil. (See Plate 31.)

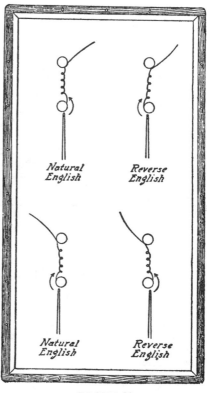

Natural English   Reverse English

Natural English   Reverse English

PLATE 30

Another point to remember that is often of great value in position play, or in getting "out of a hole," is that the effect of English *on the opposite cushion* is *opposite* to the effect on the *first* cushion. Plate No. 32 shows this point. Remember, the ball once set spinning keeps on spinning in the same way.

How Much English Will Take. — One more fact is well worth noting at this point. It is as to the amount

of English that will "take." English is transferred from
the cue ball to the object ball to any appreciable degree

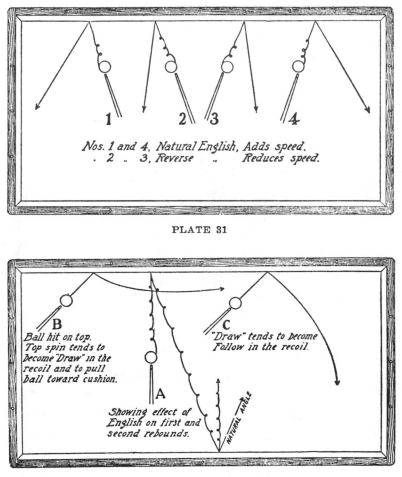

Nos. 1 and 4, Natural English, Adds speed.
. 2 .. 3, Reverse   „   Reduces speed.

PLATE 31

B
Ball hit on top.
Top spin tends to
become "Draw" in the
recoil and to pull
ball toward cushion.

C
"Draw" tends to become
Follow in the recoil.

A
Showing effect of
English on first and
second rebounds.

NATURAL ANGLE

PLATE 32

only when the cue ball strikes the object ball dead in the
center, or not far from the center. English "takes"
on a cushion in the greatest degree when that cushion is

hit most directly. In fact, when the angle of incidence is very acute the angle of reflection is very little affected by English. (See Plate 33.)

The " Dead Ball."— In modern billiards the " dead ball " is a term constantly recurring. The dead ball is a ball that " lands dead "; that is, it moves slowly when

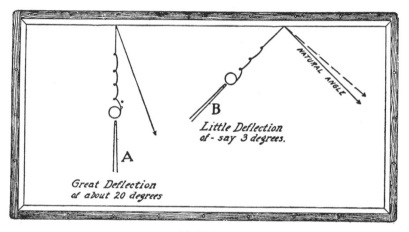

NATURAL ANGLE

B

Little Deflection of - say 3 degrees.

A

Great Deflection of about 20 degrees

PLATE 33

it comes in contact with the carom ball, and moves very little after contact, and it *does not drive the second ball away* after the completion of the carom.

To master the dead ball in all its moods and tenses is an absolute necessity in first-class position play. The dead ball is attained by hitting cue ball center and the first object ball FULL, thus giving all the life to the object ball and taking it away from the cue ball.

Plate No. 34 shows where the cue tip should strike the cue ball to get various effects, supposing in each instance that the object ball is hit in the center or very nearly so. For if it be not hit full the cue ball will not be stopped dead, no matter where the tip of the cue struck it.

Another qualification must also be made. The distance of the first object ball from the cue ball makes a difference. If the object ball be near the cue ball a center-hit cue ball will stop dead. If, however, the object ball is far away from the cue ball, the latter, in traveling the length of the table, is affected by the friction with the cloth and it must be hit a trifle below the center to overcome the cloth friction.

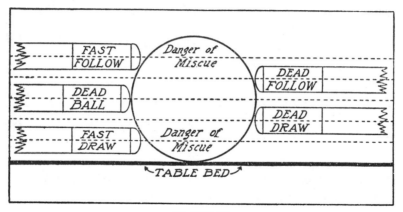

PLATE 34

The point to be accomplished is to have the cue ball strike the object ball just when it has neither forward roll from cloth friction nor backward spin from being hit below the center — when it is still sliding. When the cue ball is very near the object ball you may hit the cue ball center and get the dead ball result without allowing for cloth friction.

Again, if the sliding ceases and the forward roll begins (on a shot the full length of the table), the shot will be a "follow" from the forward roll obtained from cloth friction alone. Experts often make use of this cloth friction when the cue ball is far from both object balls and they wish to make a soft carom shot. By hitting the cue ball low it "drags," yet, having been struck with some force, it holds a direct line and does not roll off to the side from irregularity of shape in the ball, nor from pits in an old cloth. It slows up and counts softly.

A Mental Help on " Dead Ball " Shots.—If you have a right-angle or wide-angle carom which you wish to make "dead," it is frequently of mental assistance to imagine the carom ball is only two inches away from the first object ball and then make the shot as if that were really where the carom ball lay. Just so it aids in making a draw shot to imagine the cue ball is two inches farther away from the cue tip than it really is. Make the draw shot with that idea in mind and the cue tip "goes through" well and the draw takes effect.

" Deadening " on the Cushion.— Sometimes it is desired to deaden the cue ball on the cushion. This is done by using reverse English. Reverse English on a ball slows it up after contact with the cushion. Natural English makes a "live" ball. It is the constant use of the live ball that prevents many good players from becoming really first class. *The greatest difference between the mediocre and the fine billiardist lies in the use of the dead ball.*

No other one thing in billiards, unless it be the mastery of speed, the subtle appreciation of how hard a drive should be made and how softly, has so much to do with the attainment of excellence as the mastery of the dead ball, in the sense that the dead ball is one that lands on the second ball dead, or at least rapidly dying, be it ball-to-ball shot or cushion shot.

Practice Plan for the Dead Ball.— So superlatively important is the mastery of the dead ball that I suggest in Plates 35 and 36 a scheme for effective practice. Draw a twelve-inch (or smaller) circle with chalk or even the moistened finger tip on the cloth. Place the balls (Plate 35) as for a dead draw. Try the shot several times until you can count and *not knock the carom ball from the circle.*

Try the same plan for the dead follow and the dead " spread" (wide-angle carom). Make these shots repeatedly until you are NOT AFRAID to hit the object ball FULL enough to take out all its life and produce the dead ball. At first you will not hit it full enough, in the fear that you will not count, but you will soon get over that.

In Plate 36, scheme No. 1, is shown a plan for trying the dead " spread." Leave the carom ball at A. Move the object ball from one position to another, farther and farther from A. In this way you will gradually learn to make the dead spread at wider and wider distances with certainty. Scheme No. 2 is a suggestion for placing the balls for a dead drive, moving carom ball to positions A, B, and C, and object ball from a', b', c', d', to the various lengths of shot.

The object for which you practice in this plan is to gather the balls " under the hand." So do not be satisfied with merely the count. Be satisfied only when you

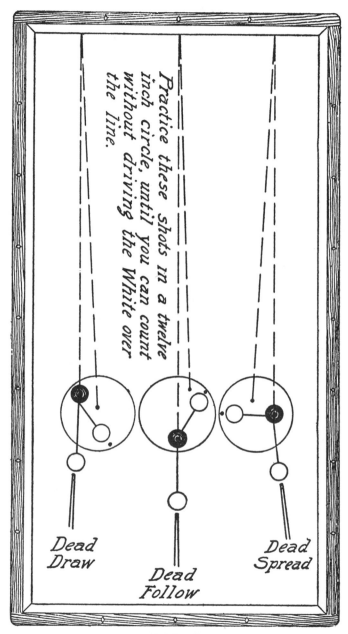

Practice these shots in a twelve inch circle, until you can count without driving the White over the line.

Dead
Draw

Dead
Follow

Dead
Spread

PLATE 35

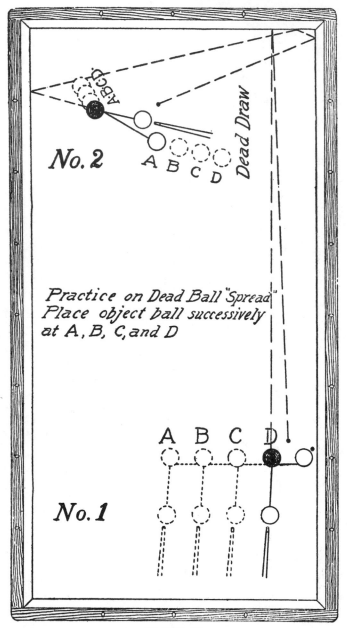

No. 2

A B C D   *Dead Draw*

Practice on Dead Ball "Spread"
Place object ball successively
at A, B, C, and D

A B C D

No. 1

PLATE 36

land dead and make the drive at just speed enough to gather all three balls in a very small space. This is the sort of practice that really counts.

The Massé Stroke.— The massé (from French, masér, to knead or rub), first developed by French experts, is a shot indispensable in modern billiards, not only as a shot with which to get out of a "hole," but with which often to play position to the best advantage.

To the neophyte it is most dazzling and incomprehensible. Yet the principles governing it are easily understood. But no other shot needs so much practice to get the exact "feel." Some assistance can be gained toward its mastery from the printed page, but practice, especially under a teacher, is almost absolutely necessary.

Do you remember when, as a boy, taking a hoop by the top, throwing it forward, but giving it a backward spin with a flip of the wrist? The hoop started forward, then the back spin caught the sidewalk and the hoop came rolling back toward you with a speed depending upon the amount of the back spin. That illustrates the principle of the massé shot. The ball acts just as the hoop acted. The back spin is put on with the cue, held upright, and striking the side of the ball in a downward stroke.

Important! The cue must not be stopped just as the ball is hit. The tip must "go through" nearly to the cloth.

Doubly important! Most beginners try to hit too near the edge. Don't strike near the edge of the cue ball, but nearer the center as you look down upon the ball. This avoids miscues. The "feel" of the shot is as though you were trying to drive the ball down through the table bed.

The Massé Bridge.— The bridge (position of the hand at the cue tip) for the ordinary massé stroke is shown in Plate 37-B. Note the palm of the bridge hand turned well forward.

Position A, in the same plate, shows the bridge for a free-hand massé, which is used when great power or a drive around the table is desired. It is not used for exact or close work if the other bridge can be made without disturbing the balls.

Plates 38 and 39 show styles of bridge used sometimes to get a firm rest when the balls are in an awkward position. These photographs are of Maurice Daly. He says these bridges were first used by Frank Ives.

The Massé Grip.— The cue may be gripped in either of two ways. They are shown in Plates 40 and 41. In No. 40 (A) the hand is turned downward; in 40 (B) it is turned upward.

For a massé grip one finger and thumb or two fingers and thumb may be used. The latter gives a firmer hold. It is well to hold the cue very firmly, but a flexible wrist motion, free from jerk, so that the cue tip may go well "through" the ball, is essential. When in position it is well to feel that the wrist is arched a bit; that makes the "follow-through" easier.

Plate 41 (A and B) shows the two grips. The ball is hit with the cue nearly perpendicular, the degree of uprightness depending upon the amount of back spin desired, and how soon you desire it to "catch," and whether you desire a short, quick curve or a longer one.

A. POSITION FOR FREE HAND POWERFUL MASSE' STROKE.

B. THE ORDINARY MASSE' BRIDGE

PLATE 37

PLATE 38

Position for massé with balls in difficult position to reach

PLATE 39

Another massé position for force massé, with balls difficult to reach

A. MR. HARRIS SHOWING CUE HAND
TURNED DOWNWARD IN MASSE SHOT.

B. HAND TURNED
UPWARD.

PLATE 40

A. THE TWO FINGER
GRIP FOR MASSE'
STROKE.

B. THE ONE FINGER
GRIP FOR
MASSE' STROKE.

PLATE 41

The diagram by Benjamin F. Garno, in "*Modern Billiards*" (Plate 42), is here reproduced by permission.

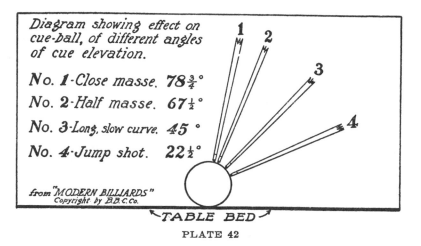

Diagram showing effect on cue-ball, of different angles of cue elevation.

No. *1-Close masse.* **78¾°**

No. *2-Half masse.* **67½°**

No. *3-Long, slow curve.* **45°**

No. *4-Jump shot.* **22½°**

from "MODERN BILLIARDS"
Copyright by B.B.C. Co.

TABLE BED

PLATE 42

Getting Aim for a Massé Shot.— Now, an important point on all close massé shots is to hit the first ball easily, land "dead" on the carom ball, and not scatter the balls. Hence, in most positions it is important to take your aim exactly as for a thin shot. (Plate 43.) The cue ball will curve and push ball No. 1 out of the way.

For close massés that will land dead (the cue ball's forward impelling force being quickly neu-

Line of aim for close Masse indicated by the arrow.

PLATE 43

tralized by the back spin) the first thing to do is to get your line of aim. Then imagine the cue ball quartered as shown in Plate No. 43. Hit the southwest (lower left) quarter, with the cue well upright. Mr. Garno says 78¾ degrees, or nearly that. Hit a good, firm stroke, and try *to feel the cue tip cling* to the cue ball, and *push* the side of the ball downward, or "knead" it down. The shot is not a sharp hammer tap, but a clinging shot. Strike *nearer the middle* of the ball than the edge and feel as though you were pushing the cue ball into the table bed.

The directions here given refer to Plate 43, with a short massé around the right of the two object balls. If the cue ball is to pass around to the left, you imagine the cue ball divided into quarters and hit the lower right (southeast) quarter.

Learn this shot well. It will serve as a basis in calculating all other massé shots. Knowing this as the normal massé, you think of others as departures from this and make calculations accordingly and execution more easy.

Thus, if the carom ball be further away from the object ball the massé effect (curvature of its course) should not take so quickly, and the cue need not be held so upright, or the cue ball need not be hit so much to the rear, but more to one side.

A Follow Massé.— Sometimes a follow shot may be effected by the massé stroke, as shown in Plate No. 44, diagram A. Or a draw shot may be made as shown in diagram B of the same plate.

The Draw Massé.— In making draw shots by massé along the cushion, hit the cue ball a wee bit on the side

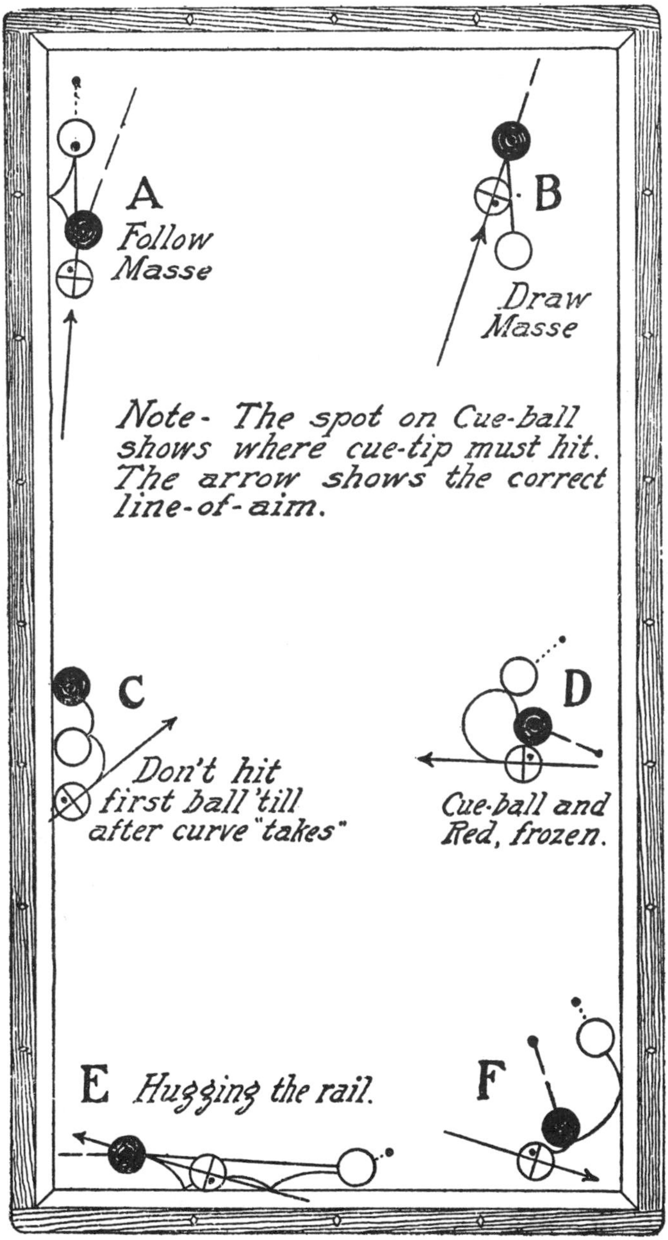

A Follow Masse

B Draw Masse

Note - The spot on Cue-ball shows where cue-tip must hit. The arrow shows the correct line-of-aim.

C Don't hit first ball'till after curve "takes"

D Cue-ball and Red, frozen.

E Hugging the rail.

F

PLATE 44

toward the cushion and the cue ball, in coming back, will "hug the rail." Plate No. 44 shows several varieties of the massé, but they are all applications of the same basic principle. The arrows show the line of original aim, the dots on the cue ball show where it should be struck by the cue tip.

Cushion Caroms.— In playing position billiards the tyro is tempted to use English on almost every shot. He must learn early never to use English unless there is a SPECIAL REASON for it. In cushion shots, more especially in one-cushion shots, avoid English if you can, thus getting the "land" much more nearly dead, as well as increasing your accuracy of execution.

Hardly another shot on the table except the draw is so productive of good positions as the one-cushion shot. If the angle is natural it is true about nine times out of ten that the shot should be played without English. The cue ball lands lightly and does not kick the carom ball away.

End of Part 1.

PART II
By Maurice Daly

FIRST PRINCIPLES OF POSITION PLAY AT BILLIARDS

By Maurice Daly

1 — Don't drive until you have to.

2 — Other things equal, the short drive is better than the long drive.

3 — Avoid a long drive of both balls.

4 — Avoid a long drive of the second object ball.

5 — Keep both balls in the " short table."

6 — A shot which leaves the cue ball far from both object balls is generally a bad shot.

7 — Along the rails choose that shot which will leave the cue ball " outside " (nearer center table) of the object balls.

8 — Keep the balls " ahead " of you.

9 — Avoid leaving cue ball frozen to the cushion.

10 — On short drives, follows, and caroms, look out for " line-ups " and " tie-ups " that come from landing on the second ball too softly.

11 — A " dead " draw, follow, or massé, is generally better than a " live " one.

12 — On open-table shots, if nothing better offers, try to leave at least one ball near a cushion, and, if possible, near a corner.

CHAPTER IV

A BSOLUTE mastery of the game of billiards is unattainable. Mastery would mean the ability to start from any given " leave " and play as long as one wished without missing. And that would take all the sport out of billiards.

Real excellence at the game, however, is attainable by the majority of players. It is an old saying that " Anyone who can learn to write can learn to draw." It is only a matter of study and practice to be able to guide the pen along certain lines rather than along others. And so with billiards. *Anyone who can play billiards at all can play better.*

Given a certain position, any player can learn that one way of making the shot is likely to prove better than another way of making it. Having learned that " position shot," he can learn another one, and so on.

Value of System in Practice.—I cannot too strenuously urge the value of system in practice. " There's a big difference in ginger," as the saying goes. Aimless knocking about of the balls will not increase your averages. When you learn a valuable shot, practice it repeatedly until it is not only mastered, but you recognize it instantly in whatever part of the table it bobs up. It becomes an old friend, and you become confident of results as soon as you see it. And confidence is of the utmost importance in billiards.

Diagrams can indicate general principles only, and not always perfectly at that; for let one alter the position of the balls the veriest trifle, in many cases, and the whole strategic character of the position is changed.

In no other game does "such a little difference make such a big difference." It is a game of "tremendous trifles." So, after reading the points here made, set the balls on the table and try the shots over and over, not only in the places indicated, but with variations therefrom.

How Frank Ives Practiced.—The late Frank C. Ives, now generally credited—and rightly, I think—with being the finest exponent of high-class competition billiards in the history of the game, would practice for hours on one thing; for instance, on working "through" the balls. I have known him to put in a week on two or three keynote shots with their variations.

Having learned a given position, subsequent play will show that the principle ruling it will serve to direct the player in any other similar position. A thorough understanding of even a few conventional position plays will really be an understanding of a great many which grow out of it.

Fundamental Errors Not Many.—A playing experience of some forty years has led me to believe that the fundamental errors of the average billiard player are not many. But they are important. One fundamental mistake causes errors in a great many places.

Some of the most fundamental principles for the

young billiard player we take up here. The accompanying diagrams are illustrations of these principles in one place on the table, and they are made from actual play. Most of them arise in many other places. Possible diagrams are innumerable, but with general principles well in mind you soon apply them instinctively in countless places. And you will learn to avoid making the shot by the wrong plan, even though the right one be a little more difficult.

It is even more important that *you do not delude yourself, even though a good position results from a badly chosen shot, that it was a good shot.* For it is not *single instances* that tell the story; it is the *average of all attempts* in like situations. Such self-delusion does more than any other one thing I know to prevent improvement in many players.

There is only a slight difference between good players and the best players, but it is that little distinguishing difference that is so difficult of mastery and so productive of results.

What Is a Good Position Shot? — That position shot is most perfect which gives the widest option of play on the following shot, and is easiest to execute perfectly "for the count." Its points of desirability are:

1 — It should give the choice of the most cushions.

2 — Those cushions should be near.

3 — The cue ball should be near (but not too near) the object balls, which should also be close together. The balls, as the phrase goes, are "under your hand."

These points of desirability are all attained only in the "short table;" that is, in the part of the table between the spots and the end rails. In mid-table, no matter how well the balls be placed for the immediate count, the player is always in danger, if the balls act the least bit badly, of losing control at once. He may make the count, but, being at mid-table, has little choice of shot, must make long drives, and generally is in danger. The *same leave near the end rail would have no dangers to speak of. The player has at least 100 per cent the best of it in the short table.*

It is related that an enthusiastic billiard tyro, upon seeing Jacob Schaefer, "The Wizard," make a long run of easy caroms, exclaimed, "Anybody can make those shots." To some extent this illustrates the difference between good and bad billiards. It may cause the blood to thrill at times to observe the pyrotechnical display, the long massé, the unnaturally angled cushion shot, the spectacular draw, but such things persisted in as a system of play, never win championships.

As a matter of fact, once the balls are "out of control" it is merely a matter of execution and luck to make the single shot; and nearly any good amateur has as good a chance (for the count) as the best professional. Good billiards lies in *avoiding the necessity of making hard shots.* That's why great players sacrifice good clusters in mid-table to get AT ONCE back to the ends. Fancy shots are a separate department of the game.

CHAPTER V

PRINCIPLE No. 1.—DON'T DRIVE (OR SHOOT HARD) TILL
YOU HAVE TO

H E IS the best performer who makes the most points,
moving the balls the least.   Here, in Plate 45 (see
both A and B) is shown how young players throw away
more chances for runs than in any other situation I now
think of.   It is when the two object balls are very near
together, the cue ball near them, and an easy carom for
the first shot.   The FIRST SHOT is the IMPORTANT
thing.   Ninety-nine times out of a hundred the tyro hits
the cue ball too hard.   It is not enough to hit the object
balls so softly that they move only three or four inches.
They must hardly move at all, no more than an inch or
so, less if possible.

In this plate (No. 45) is a special diagram (C) showing how, given proper execution, one may softly pass
the cue ball across the face of both object balls, the
object balls meantime traveling along parallel lines in
the path indicated by the dotted outline balls.   The cue
ball on each shot just *passes the center* of the second
ball, leaving the same shot on the way back.   The object
balls are hardly moved.   I have made 84 counts in a
game at this "edge" or "pass" nurse, and where can
you get any cheaper counts?   Ives has made more than
a hundred at it in the open table, and any fairly good

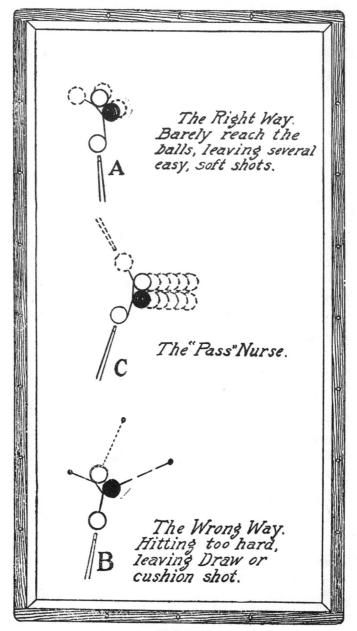

The Right Way.
Barely reach the
balls, leaving several
easy, soft shots.

A

The "Pass" Nurse.

C

The Wrong Way.
Hitting too hard,
leaving Draw or
cushion shot.

B

PLATE 45

amateur, by practice can make a good cluster before losing the position.

This is really a sort of advanced position play, but it develops so easily and naturally out of the position shown in the plate that I draw attention to it here. It is a nurse that will happen oftener for beginners than any other, and it is the basis of nursing in nearly all places. Knowing this one shot and its derivatives will make a "two-man" (average) out of almost any "one man."

The "Split" and "Going Through."—The "split" shot and other "passing-through" shots of all kinds are carefully practiced by the best players. In general the point to be attained is this: when the two object balls are being forced toward mid-table, "go through" with the cue ball and flock the object balls back toward the corners or balk-lines.

The necessity of going through arises when with the two object balls near together and *facing mid-table* the cue ball is "between" them and cannot be gotten off to the right or left to work the "edge" nurse across the face of the balls. The FIRST SHOT is THE KEY to the situation. On that all the damage is done if it be made too hard. If it is made just right, then two or three more soft ones will put the cue ball "through" and various easy position possibilities result.

Diagram A of Plate No. 46 shows the idea. Diagrams B and C are variations. In general, in this play, stay *near the second ball* at the end of each stroke. The cue ball hits one ball *less than the other*, so that motion is imparted to one only. Some special details on this play

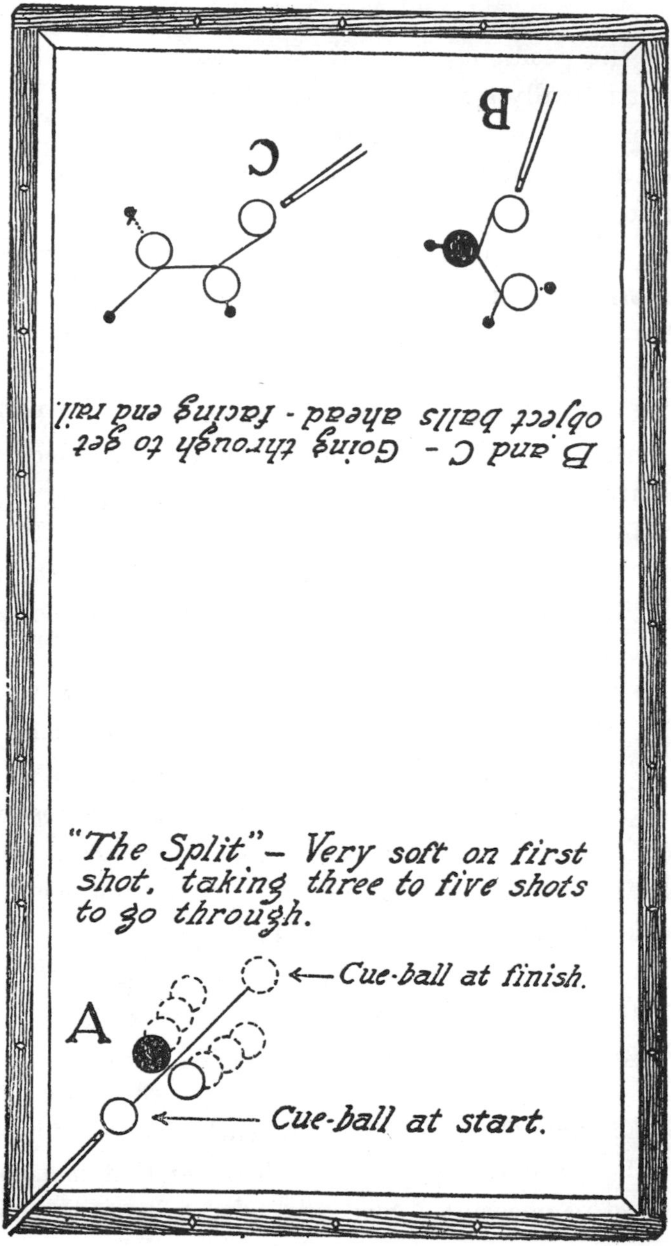

B

C

B and C - Going through to get
object balls ahead - facing end rail.

"The Split" - Very soft on first
shot, taking three to five shots
to go through.

← Cue-ball at finish.

A

← Cue-ball at start.

PLATE 46

are taken up in the chapters on "advanced position play."

In Plate 47 is shown one of the most deceptive positions to beginners and one of very frequent occurrence. The temptation is to try to drive either the first object ball twice across, following the carom ball (second object ball) which is likely to leave a line-up; or to drive the

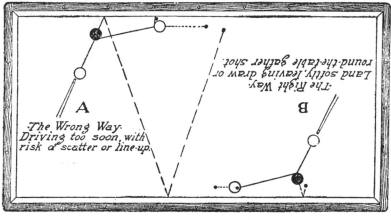

A

The Wrong Way.
Driving too soon, with
risk of scatter or line-up.

B

The Right Way:
Land softly, leaving draw or
round-the-table gather shot.

PLATE 47

carom ball, which shot (even though the two object balls are left together — and even that is doubtful) will certainly leave the cue ball far away from them.

"*Dropping On.*"— Play softly, just "dropping on" the carom ball, and the chances are much in favor of your getting an easy draw or an easy "round the table" position gather for your next. If you play hard there are a dozen ways for the shot to go wrong.

This plate illustrates three principles: "Don't drive until you have to," "Don't leave cue ball far from both object balls," and "Avoid a long drive of the second object ball."

As a matter of fact, most good position shots are in accord with more than one of the general principles we have set forth. We have in mind (all in the same shot) playing toward the "short table," keeping both balls "ahead," playing the short drive rather than the long, or not driving until we have to and keeping near at least one of the object balls. Position shots in which only one principle is concerned are comparatively rare.

Take Another Look! — In general, *whenever tempted to drive, take another look.* Then take a third look and see if some other shot will not answer.

In Plate 48 the balls are shown in position where the long drive (to the side rail, Diagram A) is the immediate temptation.

Think again! Try the shot shown in Diagram A, a soft carom off the white, leaving it in position for an easy draw on the next. Now you are *one point extra to the good* before driving.

Block Shots.—And just here is the place to call attention to the general principle of "blocking." (See Diagram B in Plate 48.) In playing from white to red land "dead" and leave the two balls *side by side, close together*, so that when the driven ball comes back from the cushion it is *blocked* by the width of two balls, a total of $4\frac{3}{4}$ inches of ivory instead of $2\frac{3}{8}$ inches. If you do not land dead on the second ball, but "kick it away," you leave a gap between them through which half of the time the returning driven ball will escape.

In this shot (and its variations are numerous in close

Don't Drive Yet — make soft shot first to get leave shown by dotted out-line.

Next shot will be a draw shown in Dia. B.

Correct way to make "draw." Block it.

PLATE 48

play near the end rail) one must pay strict attention to *the English on the cue ball.* That imparted to the driven object ball affects the course of the latter on its return

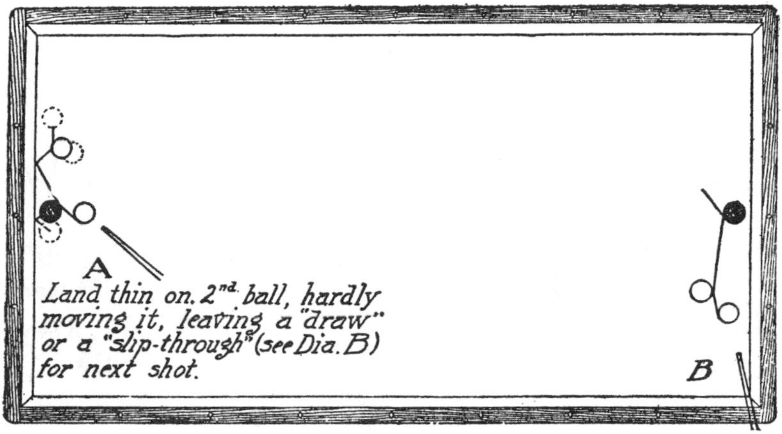

A

Land thin on. 2nd ball, hardly moving it, leaving a "draw" or a "slip-through" (see Dia. B) for next shot.

B

PLATE 49

from the cushion. This driven ball may be "thrown" one side or the other as much as three inches.

Modern Line Play and Old.— The speed of the shot should be carefully calculated, and the driven ball should, if perfectly played, *just barely get back* to the two others without kicking them away. Better not quite get back than to come back too swiftly. This will appear in more detail in "advanced position play" in considering the driven ball in playing the balk-line nurse in modern line play and its differences from the older methods.

In Plate 49 is still another example of "don't shoot hard or drive until you have to." In general, the point of the thing is to SEE WHY you do not have to, and what other way there is. With the ball as shown in **Diagram A,** if you shoot very softly, hitting the second ball thin on the far side, scarcely disturbing it, you get either another " slip through " or an easy, perfect draw shot (remember to "block" it) for position. The dotted outline balls show the new leave. In general, when the two object balls are close together *make as many soft points as you can before driving*, or going through.

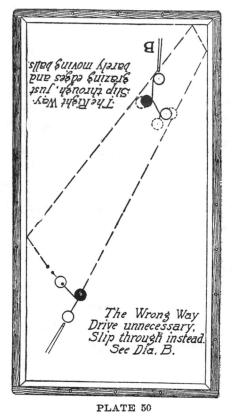

Diagram **B** shows one resulting position of the soft shot; they may vary some but seldom are bad.

The Last Few Inches.—Plate **50** shows a position where the temptation is to drive at once, and, indeed, the drive, if well made, will result in a good leave.

But — and it is a very big "but"— YOU NEVER CAN TELL ABOUT THE LAST SIX

PLATE 50

INCHES OF A LONG DRIVE. Bad "breaks" of all kinds are possible with the most skillful driver in the world. They are bound to occur, according to the law of averages. So AVOID

LONG DRIVES. In the case in question, get the easy count first (you are at least one count to the good), and you will have a short drive, or more easy caroms left, if you play as shown in the diagram.

CHAPTER VI

PRINCIPLE No. 2.—OTHER THINGS EQUAL, THE SHORT
DRIVE IS BETTER THAN THE LONG DRIVE

O NE diagram will do for illustrating this point, which
is, of course, obvious. Still I constantly see sup-
posedly good players striving to get the balls in position

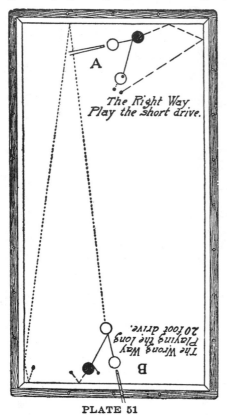

The Right Way
Play the short drive.

The Wrong Way
Playing the long
20 foot drive.

B

PLATE 51

to make a long drive
for a gather instead of
getting them in a posi-
tion to make a short
drive for the same ob-
ject.

Note especially Plate
51. The draw is equally
easy from either ball.
But in the one case the
object ball must travel
nearly twenty feet, in
the other only half of
that distance. Take
the short drive in pref-
erence to the long
drive. It is easier to
control the resulting
leave. No matter how
attractive a long drive
may appear, you *can-
not tell about its last few inches.* And in position play
they are the inches that count most.

72

CHAPTER VII

PRINCIPLE No. 3.—AVOID A LONG DRIVE OF BOTH BALLS

THE temptation to drive both balls arises most frequently when it seems that by so doing both object balls can be gathered near a corner. The danger points of such a shot are: First, the difficulty of landing exactly right on the second ball, a perfect "land" being very doubtful at a range of more than a foot; secondly, the fact that even though you make the count as you planned you leave the cue ball *far from both object balls*, and, thirdly, there is the danger of a "tie-up" through lining the balls or by freezing to the cushion.

In a recent championship match one of our foremost players

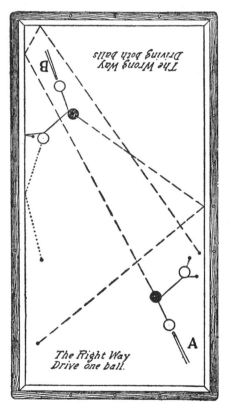

The Wrong Way
Driving both balls

The Right Way
Drive one ball.

PLATE 52

73

several times came to a halt in his run through difficulties resulting (a couple of shots before) from a drive of both balls to get them near a corner. In another championship tournament the loss of the game, and probably the championship, was directly traceable to this mistaken tactic. In one game this player made five such attempts, and four of them failed to produce a satisfactory result. One of them left him badly "tied up," and his resulting miss left his opponent a fine leave from which a long run resulted.

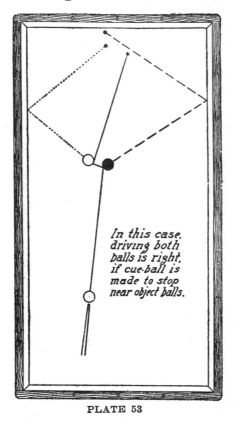

In this case, driving both balls is right, if cue-ball is made to stop near object balls.

PLATE 53

THE PERCENTAGE IS AGAINST YOU WHENEVER YOU TRY A LONG DRIVE OF BOTH BALLS, with this solitary exception, when after such a drive you can leave the cue ball near, or fairly near, the other two.

In Plate No. 52, Diagram A, is shown a frequent position and the right way to play it. The temptation for the beginner is to drive both balls to the far right-hand corner. But if he does this he leaves the cue ball far from both object balls and there is the chance of a line-up. There is the chance of not getting them both in the short table. There is the chance of hitting the first ball too softly, or too hard, or too thin. In driving *one* ball there is not half the chance to go wrong. Diagram A shows the right way to make the shot, Diagram B the wrong way to make it.

There are, of course, some exceptions, no generalization being wholly true.

When Both Balls May Be Driven.—In addition to the exception noted, when the cue ball can be made to stop near the others, is this, that *short* drives of both balls may be safely made. A short drive means one of a foot or so, seldom more. Or such a shot can be made *as a last resort* in a bad place; for instance, when the balls must be gotten out of balk.

A

The Wrong Way - A fast draw, driving both balls.

The Right Way - A "dead" draw with resulting gather.

B

PLATE 54

Plate 53 shows an example where both balls may be driven, because the cue ball may be made to stop *near* the *other two.*

Sometimes the beginner "drives both balls" and loses a good position through not suspecting he is driving the second ball, because the shot is a draw, and he makes a "live" draw, landing at speed instead of "dead" on the second ball. Plate 54 shows such a happening. Diagram A shows the wrong way, Diagram B the right way of making the shot.

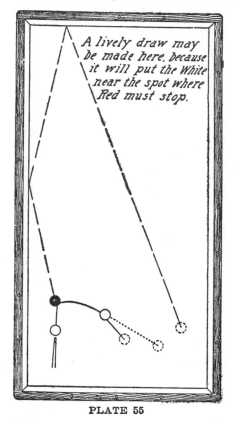

A lively draw may be made here, because it will put the White near the spot where Red must stop.

PLATE 55

This again suggests an exception. There are times (though very, very rare) when the fast draw is the better shot. Plate 55 shows such a case. But in general all these draw shots, and especially where the drive of the first object ball is long, *find where that is going to stop,* and try to land the carom ball, and, if possible, the cue ball, too, near the same point.

Importance of Correct Speed.—There is nothing in billiards, not even the choice of shots, that is of more importance than getting the exact amount of force, so the balls may land "under the hand." They must, if possible, be in a little cluster, where they are absolutely

under control, not merely " somewhere near " each other.
Four or five inches of separation is *big*. The expert
wants them an *inch* apart if possible. No matter how
good a selection of shot be made, if it is much overdone
or underdone it is not much better than making the
wrong shot.

It is in this wonderful control of force that the principal superiority of Willie Hoppe's game exists. His
line nursing, or nursing of any other description, rarely
runs into large figures. But on his gather shots he puts
them " under his hand " ; that is, all huddled closely
together.

CHAPTER VIII

PRINCIPLE No. 4.—AVOID A LONG DRIVE OF THE SEC-
OND OBJECT BALL

PLATE No. 56 depicts a characteristic leave where
the temptation comes to one to drive the second
object ball. Diagram A shows how to try it. Shoot
softly, just "dropping on" the second ball, leaving the
first object ball near the cushion. Then you get either
an easy draw for position or an easy cushion shot for a
gather in the corner, the second ball being a "big ball."

What Is a "Big Ball"?—A "big ball" means an
object ball lying near a cushion or cushions in such position that the cue ball approaching it for a carom may
hit it either directly or on the rebound from one of the
cushions. For instance, on a round-the-table shot, if
the second ball lies down in the corner about three inches
from both sides of the "jaw," the ball is nearly a "foot
big." That is, the cue ball may enter the corner anywhere within the range of a foot, and the count will be
made, because it cannot escape counting either directly
or on the rebound.

Lansing Perkins holds that any ball, no matter where
it lies is 7 inches "big." Place the three balls frozen,
side by side in a line, and it is $7\frac{1}{8}$ inches from the outside
to the outside of the two balls on the end. I figure it
differently, however. I measure from the center to cen-

ter of the two outside balls; that is, from the path or line on which they roll. This gives twice the width of one ball, or $4\frac{6}{8}$ inches. An approaching cue ball coming anywhere within that $4\frac{6}{8}$-inch path is bound to hit the object ball. So it may lend you confidence to know when attempting a difficult shot that the ball is really $4\frac{3}{4}$ inches wide instead of $2\frac{3}{8}$ inches, its own diameter. But this is wandering from our diagram (56).

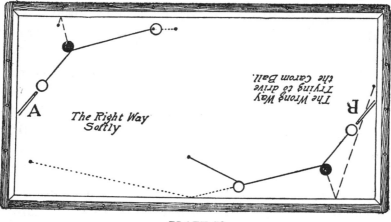

The Right Way
Softly

The Wrong Way
Trying to drive
the Carom Ball.

PLATE 56

Diagram B shows the wrong way and one of the possible bad results. The other possible bad results are numerous. Generally the result from playing the shot correctly (A) is a draw.

Value of the Draw Shot.—And here is a general rule —

AN EASY DRAW IN "BALL-TO-BALL" BILLIARDS IS ONE OF THE BEST LEAVES POSSIBLE TO GET.

The draw, in fact, is the keynote shot of ball-to-ball

billiards. Frank Ives held that the secret of balk-line billiards lay in the draw and massé. "In case of doubt, draw," he said. And while that may be too broad for absolute application, it is nevertheless indicative of the importance and value of the stroke, and oftener than not the correct procedure.

In golf they say "the man who can putt can beat anybody." In billiards the man who can draw and massé well is always dangerous. If in addition to that he has good control of one-cushion shots, always very valuable in position play possibilities, he is a dangerous opponent.

Getting the Thin Shot.— Keep in mind always the plan of leaving the balls for a draw, or for a thin shot, and then a draw. The "thin shot," too, is a valuable one and will be taken up in detail later on. But this may be said here: The "thin shot" leave is also likely to leave the option of a half follow. Play half follow *when going toward the corners* or to the short table from a mid-table position. When already in the short table, and looking toward the side rails, the thin shot and then a draw is more often the better plan.

CHAPTER IX

PRINCIPLE No. 5.— KEEP THE BALLS IN THE "SHORT TABLE"

I N Plate 57 is shown the table, with lines drawn across it intersecting the two spots. Between these lines and the end rails is the territory known as "the short table." The rest of the field is "mid-table" or "center table."

Plate 58 illustrates a frequent and a characteristic situation where a draw shot from either object ball is a

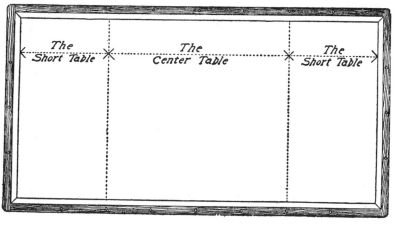

PLATE 57

"gather" shot. But the shot should be made as indicated to gather the balls in the "short table," rather than to draw from the other ball, even though in this case it is

81

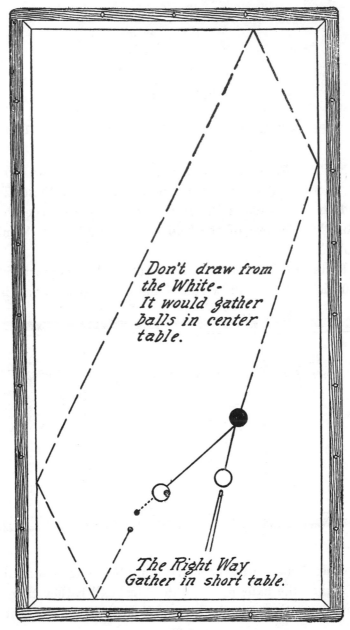

Don't draw from the White - It would gather balls in center table.

The Right Way Gather in short table.

PLATE 58

a long drive in preference to a short drive. The *most important* thing is to keep the balls *toward the end rails* where, in case the balls act badly, *more opportunities for recovery exist*. In making such shots as this, make every effort to so regulate the speed of the shot that the balls may gather "under your hand."

Plate 59 illustrates again the same principle. A draw from either ball will be a "gather," but one gathers in

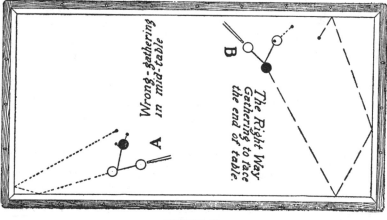

PLATE 59

the short table, the other in mid-table. Keeping the balls towards the end rails overrules almost everything else, except that attempting too difficult a shot is not advisable. Making the count is, of course, the first rule in competitions. With a fair chance for a good result always choose the sure shot over the doubtful one.

Plate 60 is to the same point, but the first shot is preparatory, while the "gather" is on the second shot.

In this plate, Diagram A looks toward a gather in the short table, B toward a gather in mid-table. There is a great variety of such situations.

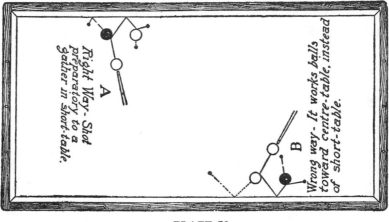

PLATE 60

Plate 61 shows one of the most frequent positions in which the beginner is likely to go astray. In his haste

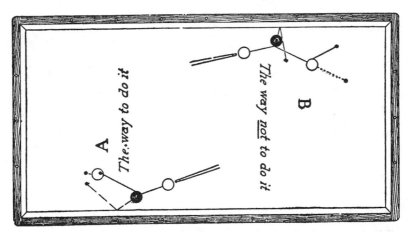

PLATE 61

to make the count he blazes away for a simple ball-to-ball carom, hitting the first object ball thin, makes the count, but "loses" the balls. Diagram A shows the way the shots should have been made: a half follow shot, so as to carry both balls along together, keeping them "ahead" of you, and even putting them into the short table. Diagram B shows the way not to do it.

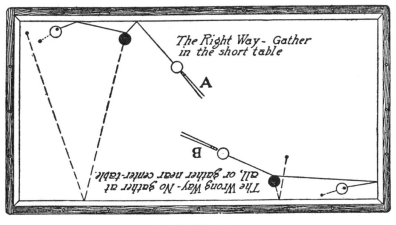

PLATE 62

Plate 62, Diagram A, shows a " cushion-first " shot, resulting in a gather in the short table. By playing on the ball first, as shown in Diagram B, there is no gather at all, and the best one can hope for is that they get together somewhere in "the open sea" of mid-table.

Shifting of English.— Most beginners are quick to learn the effect of English on the right or left sides of the cue ball. They are slower to appreciate even in simple shots the important difference (in effect on the cue ball's course after striking a cushion) between " top "

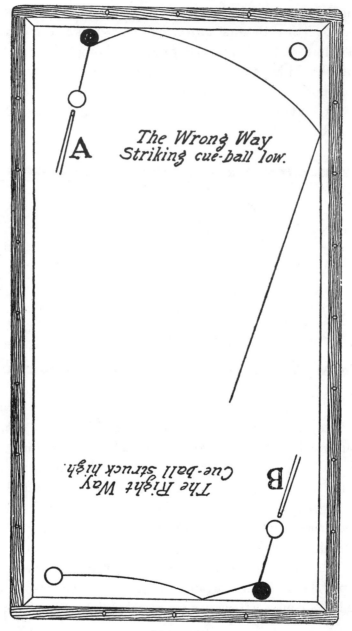

The Wrong Way
Striking cue-ball low.

The Right Way
Cue-ball struck high.

PLATE 63

and "bottom" (draw or follow) English. Bear in mind that when a ball is hit low with the cue it comes back from the cushion with that underspin still effective, and on its *new course* (from an OPPOSITE cushion) the underspin is no longer acting as draw but as follow. When a ball hit high comes off the opposite cushion the "top" is still effective, but on the ball's *new course* off the opposite cushion the original "top" is acting as "draw." It will tend to curve the ball in toward the cushion again.

A mastery of these two points is indispensable in cushion play. It is often of the greatest value in three-cushion caroms. So right here let us consider plates (63 and 64) illustrating this important point.

Plate 64 shows the opposite effect from that shown in Diagram B of Plate 63. The shot looks impossible to beginners. But let one strike the first ball thin, with plenty of "draw," and the cue ball will "swell out," as we term it; i. e., take a curved course to the corner.

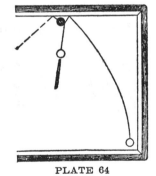

PLATE 64
Cue ball hit as for a draw

Hitting high on the same shot would send the cue ball much farther to the right, *curving toward* the end rail, as shown by the shorter dotted line.

Plate 65 shows three positions in which the second object ball (white) alone is changed. In A it is behind the first object ball. In B it is out from the cushion at right angles. In C it is forward.

In A you hit the cue ball low, in B you hit it center of ball, in C you hit it high. This illustrates forcibly the difference in effect between "top" and "bottom" Eng-

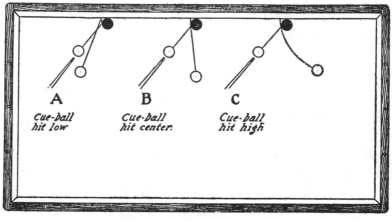

A
Cue-ball hit low

B
Cue-ball hit center.

C
Cue-ball hit high

PLATE 65

lish, which is just as great and just as important as the difference between right and left English.

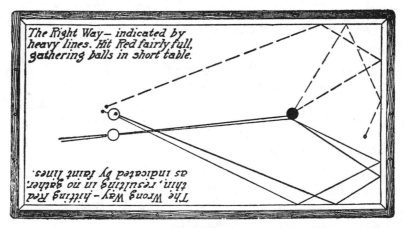

The Right Way— indicated by heavy lines. Hit Red fairly full, gathering balls in short table.

The Wrong Way – hitting Red thin, resulting in no gather, as indicated by faint lines.

PLATE 66

On the opening shot one should try to gather the balls in the short table. Plate No. 66 shows two ways of making the shot. The solid lines show the course of cue and object balls when the object ball is hit fairly full, resulting in a gather in the short table. The dotted lines show the course of cue and object balls when the object ball is hit thin, resulting in no gather at all.

CHAPTER X

PRINCIPLE No. 6.—A SHOT WHICH LEAVES THE CUE
BALL FAR FROM BOTH OBJECT BALLS IS GEN-
ERALLY A BAD SHOT

IT IS astonishing how numerous the positions are
where this principle is to be borne in mind. In a
majority of cases the execution secret is in hitting the
first ball *fuller* so as to *deaden* the cue ball and land
softly on the carom ball. Sometimes, however, it is simply a case of "shoot softly!"

A frequent leave that results in a "scatter" and the
close of the run where it might result in a gather and
continuation of play with the balls in control is shown in
Plate 67, Diagrams A and B showing the wrong and
right ways, respectively, of playing the shot.

Another frequent leave, where the "dead" cue ball is
indicated, is shown in Plate 68. Diagram B shows the
way a lively cue ball will destroy what otherwise would
have been a good position shot. The player has hit the
first object ball too thin, thus failing to deaden the cue
ball, which, returning from the cushion at speed, "kicks"
the carom ball away from a good position.

Diagram A shows a better way to make this shot, as it
deadens the cue ball, drives the first object ball around
the table and leaves the balls in the "short table," and
frequently so clustered that a simple shot or two will
place the balls in perfect position for nursing along the

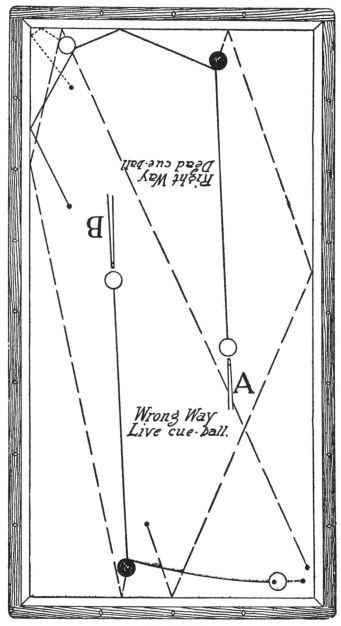

Right Way
Dead cue-ball.

B

A

Wrong Way
Live cue-ball.

PLATE 67

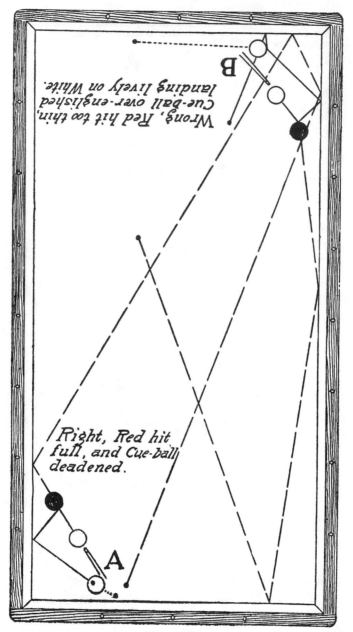

Wrong, Red hit too thin.
Cue-ball over-englished
landing lively on White.

B

Right, Red hit
full, and Cue-ball
deadened.

A

PLATE 68

rail into the corners, or, in balk-line billiards, along the line.

It is the judicious selection of such opportunities, not the execution of remarkable shots, that determines whether you will make one or two points, or a run of some proportions.

Deadening on the Cushion. — Frequently it is necessary to deaden the cue ball on the cushion, instead of on the object ball. Plate 69 shows three examples of this. Diagram A may need a little explanation. To get the red ball around the corner and out to join the other two, instead of hitting it thin, having it return along the end rail, you hit it full. Then the cue ball "follows" it some. But the *right* English brings the cue ball back again, *deadened* to the carom ball, avoiding knocking it away to some undesirable position.

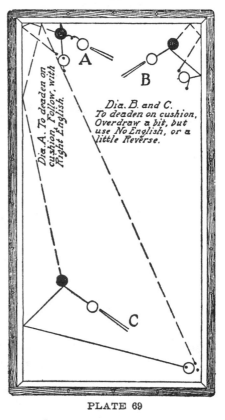

Dia. A. To deaden on cushion. Follow, with Right English.

Dia. B. and C.
To deaden on cushion, Overdraw a bit, but use No English, or a little Reverse.

PLATE 69

In Diagram B the cue ball is deadened on the side rail, as it is also in Diagram C. If these shots were played with natural English, the resulting lively ball would kick the carom ball away and "control" would go glimmering.

Plate 70 shows another kind of a leave where nevertheless the idea is to keep the cue ball near the carom ball on completion of the shot. Diagram A shows the path of the shot pointed by "The Tempter." It is the most natural thing in the world to hit the object ball well on the right, with "right draw" English. The

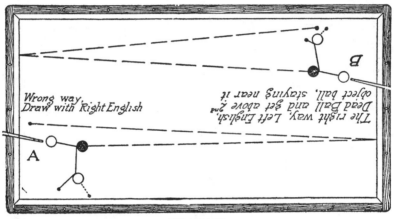

PLATE 70

better way (a favorite shot of Willie Hoppe) is "the dead ball," with left English, the cue ball just passing the carom ball and *staying near it*. The result is a position from which an easy gather can almost always be made. This is a typical example, too, of staying near at least one object ball. *If you cannot "hold" one of them, hold the other.*

In Plate 71 we see a frequent draw shot with no quickly apparent position play. By *staying near the carom ball* the object ball may be made to stop anywhere within the curved line on the diagram and a gather shot

61

be generally possible, either by draw, " spread draw," or cushion shot.

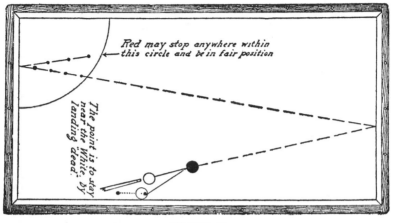

Red may stop anywhere within this circle and be in fair position

The point is to stay near the White, by landing dead.

PLATE 71

Plate 72 depicts a characteristic position, which has many slight variations, with the same principle applying throughout. By playing the natural angle and no English you land " dead " and gather the balls. The Eng-

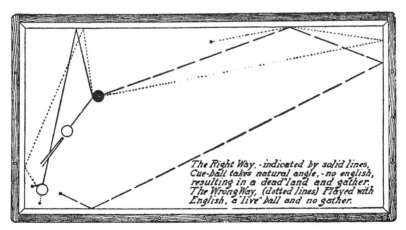

The Right Way, indicated by solid lines, Cue-ball takes natural angle, no english, resulting in a dead land and gather. The Wrong Way, (dotted lines) Played with English, a 'live' ball and no gather.

PLATE 72

lish "live" ball may be more certain to count, but it is almost certain to spoil the gather. This applies to three-quarters of the cross table one-cushion shots.

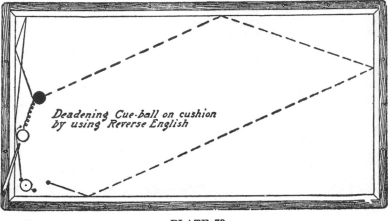

Deadening Cue-ball on cushion by using Reverse English

PLATE 73

Plate 73 shows one modification of this leave in which the end rail may be taken by the cue ball first. The cue ball, on taking the second cushion, is held back to

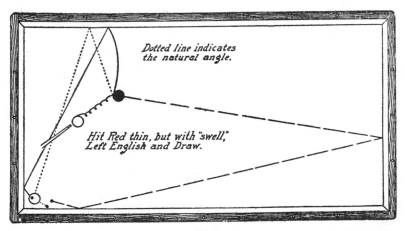

Dotted line indicates the natural angle.

Hit Red thin, but with "swell," Left English and Draw.

PLATE 74

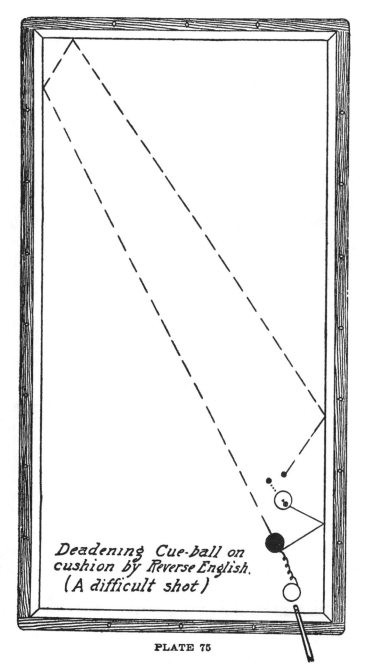

Deadening Cue-ball on
cushion by Reverse English.
(A difficult shot)

PLATE 75

the corner by the left English. This enables you to hit the object ball thin enough to get it back for a gather. The shot occurs frequently, and is very useful in its numerous variations.

Another variation of it is shown in Plate 74. Here the object ball is hit thin enough to send it up the table and back. The cue ball is hit on the "lower left-hand corner." It "swells," as shown by the curved line. The English is just sufficient to bring it slowly back to the carom ball for a soft count.

By hitting the object ball thin enough to get the drive on the proper line the cue ball will necessarily land on the side rail well above the point of a natural angle. The draw and English bring it back, but it has been "deadened on the cushion."

Plate 75 gives another illustration of deadening on the cushion. The right English does it. The leave is so common, and beginners so seldom play it correctly, that the diagram ought to be useful.

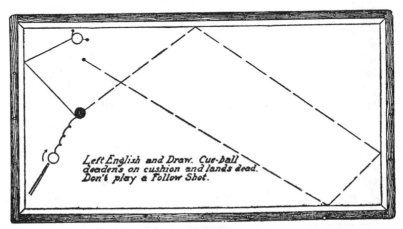

Left English and Draw. Cue-ball deadens on cushion and lands dead. Don't play a Follow Shot.

PLATE 76

One more example of this deadening on the cushion. Plate 76 shows it. Nine times out of ten the beginner goes for the follow shot. He probably counts, but the balls are gone. Now, by playing the cue ball with draw and left English over to the end rail he can count and land dead, at the same time driving the object ball around for position.

CHAPTER XI

PRINCIPLE No. 7.—ALONG THE RAIL, CHOOSE THAT SHOT WHICH WILL LEAVE THE CUE BALL "OUT-SIDE" (NEARER MID-TABLE) OF THE OBJECT BALLS

AMONG players one hears a great deal about "system." If that word, as used, means anything exact and definite, which I sometimes doubt, it refers as much

The Wrong Way·
Landing on inside edge.

The Right Way·
Landing on outside of center

PLATE 77

as anything to the point of keeping the two object balls "ahead" of the cue ball; that is, "pointed" toward the end rail or nearest cushion, rather than toward mid-table, the "open sea." Sometimes one shot brings the desired result. Sometimes the first, or even the second and third shots, are preparatory only. But the principle is plain and well illustrated in Plate 77, a position in which the object to be attained is so obvious that it is difficult to see

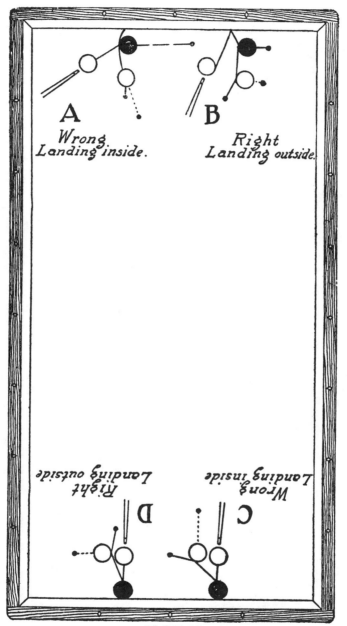

PLATE 78

A   Wrong

Cue-ball landing inside,
leaving a long drive.

A soft Follow, landing
outside of White,

Right   B

PLATE 79

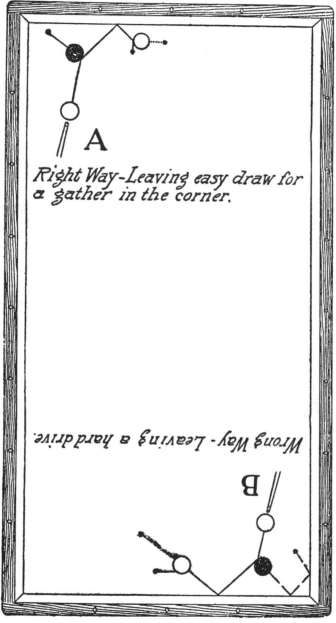

A

Right Way-Leaving easy draw for a gather in the corner.

Wrong Way - Leaving a hard drive.

B

PLATE 80

how anyone could overlook it. Yet beginners seldom try for the proper shot.

Diagram A shows what they almost always try to do, leaving the next shot a sure " scatter," with the chances against the balls being again brought under control.

Study well plates 78 and 79, which also illustrate the point of " keeping outside." Countless variations of this arise. Keep your eyes open for this object at all times, and especially when the balls are close enough

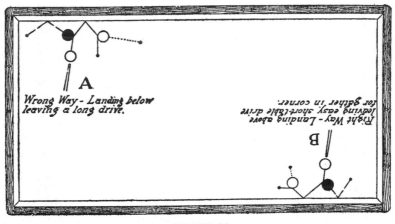

Wrong Way - Landing below leaving a long drive.

Right Way - Landing above leaving easy, short-table drive for gather in corner.

PLATE 81

together to enable you to " land " on either side of the carom ball at will without taking dangerous chances.

The mentioned plates (77, 78, and 79) are illustrative of points perhaps more properly considered under the chapter on " Second Ball Play "; but the positions shown here are so simple and common that any beginner can execute them. They are primary points of " second ball play." Advanced points will be taken up later.

Plates 80 and 81 show two more simple and frequent variations of this, but having the factor of a cushion intervening. In each case the idea is to leave easy, short drives or follows instead of long drives and "scatters."

CHAPTER XII

PRINCIPLE No. 8.— KEEP BOTH BALLS "AHEAD" OF YOU

THIS heading includes all shots where the principal point is the "carry along" of the first object ball to join the second. It may be an easy "ball-to-ball" shot, or any of the countless varieties of cushion shots. Let us consider the primary ones first.

Plate 82 shows perhaps the most frequent leave of the kind in which the beginner goes wrong.

Plate 83 shows another position where the "carry along" is generally the best shot, leaving the balls "ahead."

Plate 84 is important. It depicts a frequent leave where the kiss shot, carrying object ball along to carom ball, is the shot to give the best result, though the spread

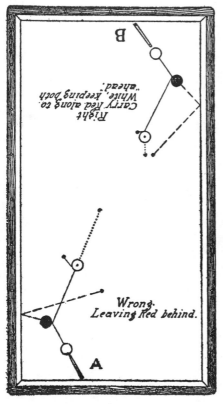

Right
Carry Red along to
White, keeping both
ahead.

Wrong.
Leaving Red behind.

PLATE 82

106

draw or cushion follow may be easier to execute for the single count.

The " Turning the Corner " Shot.— One of the really

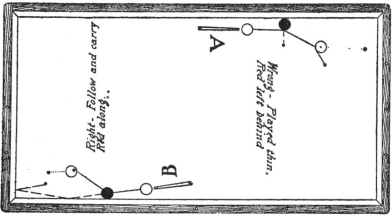

PLATE 83

valuable shots to be thoroughly familiar with, both in straight rail, balk-line, or cushion caroms, is known as the "turning the corner" shot, *fully* illustrated in

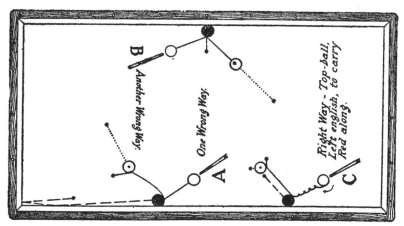

PLATE 84

Plate 85.   Diagram A shows the wrong, B the right
way.   C is the same species of shot, but at longer range.

The point of the shot is to **HIT THE OBJECT
BALL FULL** instead of hitting it thin, using enough
"top" English to bring the cue ball out to the carom
ball.   The object ball, in the meantime, having "turned
the corner" (because it was hit full), joins the other two.

The shot is one that takes practice, for the angles are
highly varied, the ranges differ greatly in length.   Not

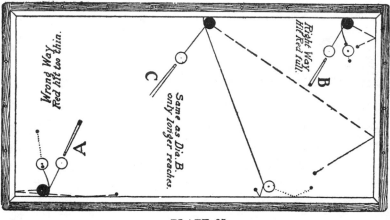

PLATE 85

only must one have the English right, be it "top" or
"bottom," or none at all, or right or left, but the speed
of the stroke must also be correct.   If the speed be too
great, it results in loss of control, and too low speed
gives an awkward leave.   But it is the mastery of such
shots as this that gives the good player opportunities to
make big runs.   It is the mastery of such details as this
that makes the difference between the "two-man" and
the "five-man."   Sometimes you see a fine player make

a very wry face after a shot of this sort when it did not land exactly as he wished, though to the average unthinking player the count was made and the balls are still near together, and there's apparently "nothing to kick about."

Balls Frozen to the Cushion. — Sometimes the beginner in billiards finds the first object ball snugly resting against a cushion — " frozen." He experiences that tired feeling and says, " Tough Luck! " But in many instances the leave is really a good one, and kiss shots off the railed balls are a part of every good player's repertoire. Many of them are real position shots, and a little practice will soon make one face such shots with perfect confidence.

In Plate 86, Diagrams A, B, and C show the object ball in three different places along the rail. To the novice the shot looks difficult. It is really not very difficult, and the balls gather if executed properly.

Shoot at moderate speed and follow the directions in the drawing. Diagram D is a modification in which the same principle rules. In all of them the idea is to " carry along" the object ball to the carom ball.

Plate 87 shows another " carry along" shot.

If the first ball were hit, then it would be left behind. Such shots bob up all over the table. It is, in fact, the idea in nearly all cushion carom gathers, especially of the round-the-table variety: Plate 88 shows one of the most frequent of this class.

Plates 89, 90, and 91 are the most frequent leaves where the " carry along" is not only essential but easily done, though often overlooked by beginners. The variations, of course, are many.

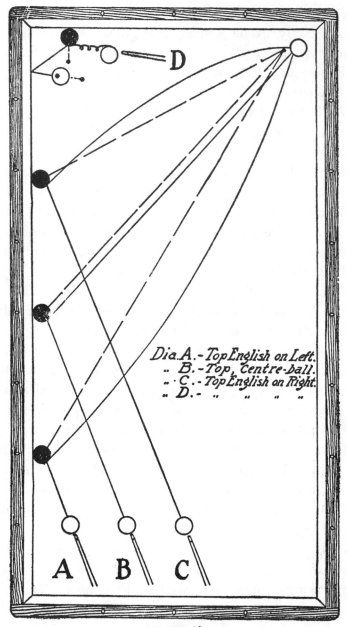

Dia. A. - Top English on Left.
" B. - Top, Centre-ball.
" C. - Top English on Right.
" D. - " " " "

A B C

D

PLATE 86

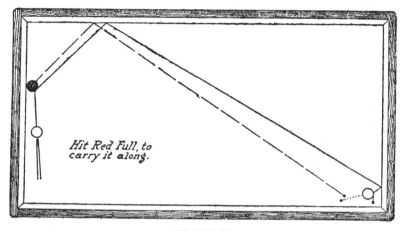

Hit Red Full, to carry it along.

PLATE 87

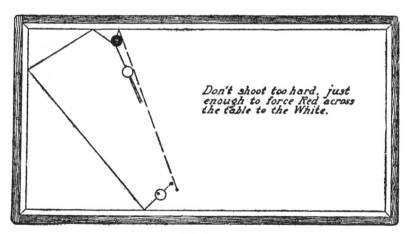

Don't shoot too hard, just enough to force Red across the table to the White.

PLATE 88

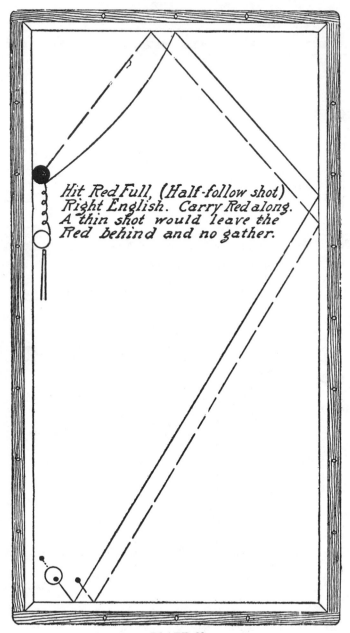

Hit Red Full, (Half-follow shot)
Right English. Carry Red along.
A thin shot would leave the
Red behind and no gather.

PLATE 89

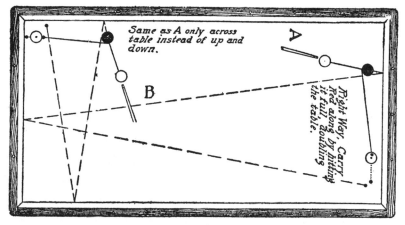

Same as A only across table instead of up and down.

A

B

Right Way. Carry Red along by hitting it full, doubling the table.

PLATE 90

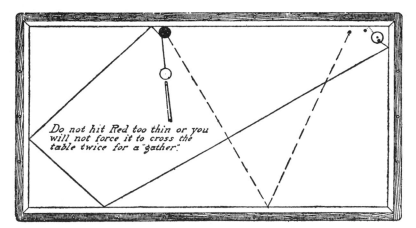

Do not hit Red too thin or you will not force it to cross the table twice for a "gather."

PLATE 91

CHAPTER XIII

PRINCIPLE No. 9.—AVOID LEAVING CUE BALL "FROZEN" TO THE CUSHION

WHEN a cue ball is frozen to the cushion much less can be done with it, for the simple and sufficient reason that you cannot cue it wherever you like. As a rule, this can be guarded against only when the cue ball has a short road to travel to the count. Hence it is not subject for much diagram exposition. One example will suffice. See Plate No. 92.

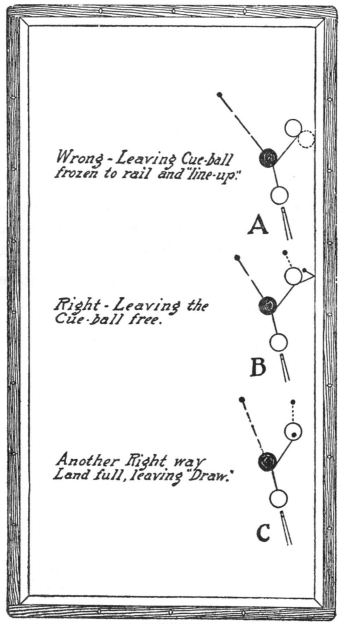

Wrong - Leaving Cue-ball frozen to rail and "line-up."

A

Right - Leaving the Cue-ball free.

B

Another Right way Land full, leaving "Draw."

C

PLATE 92

CHAPTER XIV

PRINCIPLE No. 10.— ON SHORT FOLLOWS, DRIVES AND CAROMS, LOOK OUT FOR "LINE-UPS" AND "TIE-UPS" THAT COME FROM LANDING ON THE SECOND BALL TOO SOFTLY

HERE, again, the "freeze," "line-up," and "tie-up" can be avoided in close play by a little care and imaginative foresight. It is merely a matter of get-

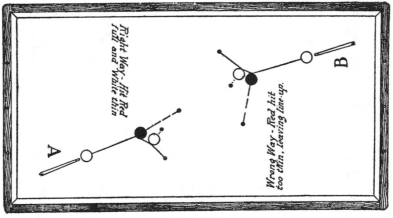

PLATE 93

ting the force of the stroke right. Plate 93 shows a position where nearly all beginners line the balls up. They try to hit the ball very thin, and either miss it entirely, or count and leave a line-up. This is shown in B. Try rather to hit the first ball a wee bit FULLER than

116

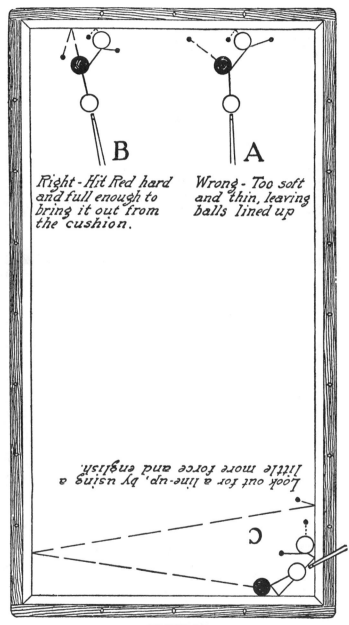

B

Right - Hit Red hard
and full enough to
bring it out from
the cushion.

A

Wrong - Too soft
and thin, leaving
balls lined up

Look out for a line-up, by using a
little more force and english.

C

PLATE 94

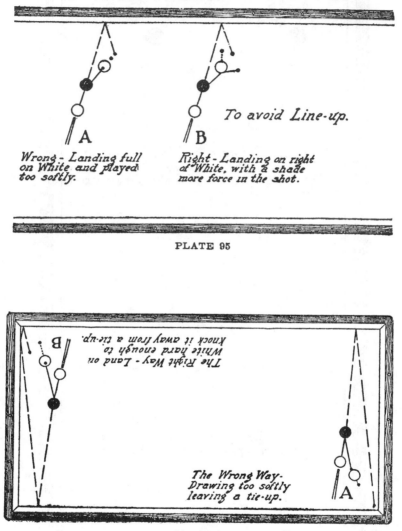

To avoid Line-up.

A

Wrong - Landing full on White and played too softly.

B

Right - Landing on right of White, with a shade more force in the shot.

PLATE 95

The Right Way - Land on White hard enough to knock it away from a tie-up.

B

The Wrong Way - Drawing too softly leaving a tie-up.

A

PLATE 96

the second, just barely grazing the second, in fact, and hardly stirring it. The first ball will move out a bit and result in a favorable position, with balls facing the corner. This shot will take considerable practice, simple as it looks, for you will be so afraid of missing the second that you will not hit the first full enough. Practice it till you overcome that fear. This, too, is important. This shot often enables you to get on the other side of the balls, so that you will be facing the corner.

Plate 94 shows an obvious example of avoiding a " line-up." Playing too softly, as in Diagram A, lines the balls on the rail. A little more force, but not enough to scatter the balls, brings the first object ball out from the rail again. Diagram C shows a frequent position where the line-up is to be avoided by using slightly more force and a trifle more English.

Plate 95 also illustrates a like point. In this case, however, one can avoid the line-up not only by using a shade more force, but by landing on the carom ball a wee bit farther to the right.

Plate 96 shows how the player drives the object ball across the table and back. The amount of force needed to drive a ball a certain distance is known sub-consciously, perhaps. On such shots as these, we, without thinking, use about so much force, learned by experience. But that amount will often line the balls up on the rail. Whenever confronted by this leave, stop a moment and then use just the least bit more force or a wee bit less than usual. Preferably, generally use a *little more*. This will be determined largely by the length of draw or the angle, even slight variations making

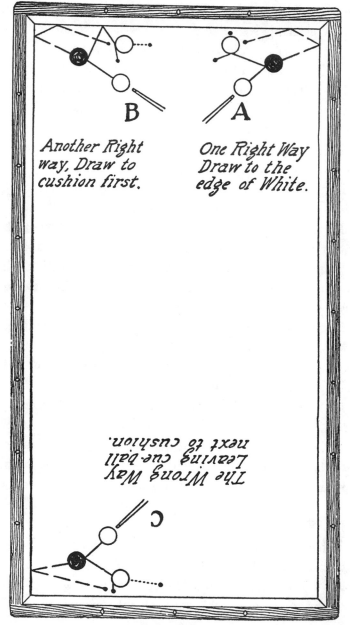

B

Another Right
way, Draw to
cushion first.

One Right Way
Draw to the
edge of White.

A

The Wrong Way
Leaving cue-ball
next to cushion.

C

PLATE 97

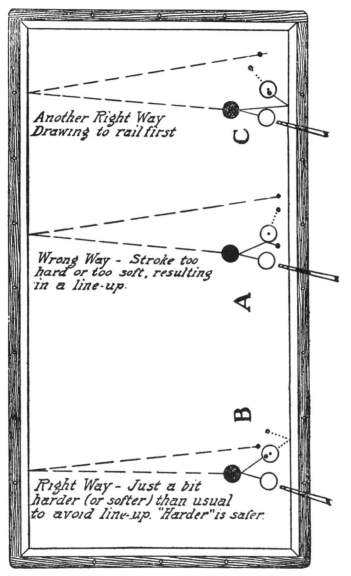

Another Right Way
Drawing to rail first

C

Wrong Way - Stroke too
hard or too soft, resulting
in a line-up.

A

B

Right Way - Just a bit
harder (or softer) than usual
to avoid line-up. "Harder" is safer.

PLATE 98

important differences that practice alone leads one to appreciate.

Diagrams A, B, and C of Plates 97 and 98 are variations of shots where players line the balls up oftener, perhaps, than anywhere else.

Of the many instances in the average game where tie-ups (generally in the form of an alignment of the balls)

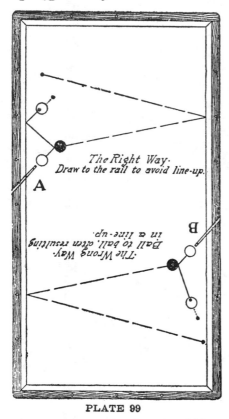

The Right Way.
Draw to the rail to avoid line-up.

A

The Wrong Way.
Ball to ball, after resulting in a line-up.

B

PLATE 99

are threatened, perhaps none is more common than the position depicted in Plate 99. It looks so simple and inviting, just an easy little "spread" shot (that is, a draw at or about a right angle). Through long practice the player almost unconsciously hits the object ball just hard enough to send it across the table and back to or very near the side rail. In this case the plain ball-to-ball "spread" is likely to result in an alignment along the rail, as shown in Diagram Γ of the same plate. It is easily avoided by drawing the ball to the cushion. Thus the object ball is kept away from the cushion, and even if

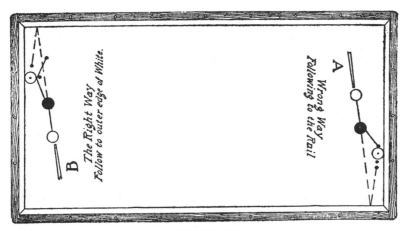

PLATE 100

they line up the cushion is available for assistance on the next shot.

In nursing balls in the short table, especially with short draw shots along the end rail, a little carelessness often results in tie-ups. I wish to give two frequent examples of this in Plates 100 and 101. Plate 100

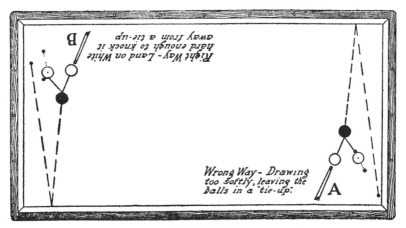

PLATE 101

shows a frequent little follow shot. Take great pains to land *on the outer edge* of the carom ball; otherwise you will be left in line with a difficult massé or scattering around the table shot. Diagram B of the same plate shows how to make the shot. These, like all close position shots, require a nicety of execution.

Plate 101 shows another threatened tie-up. By drawing the ball too slowly, just getting to the carom ball, you are likely to leave a line-up, a freeze, or a massé shot at best. This is shown in Diagram A. Diagram B shows how, by landing a little harder, you escape the threatened tie-up.

CHAPTER XV

PRINCIPLE No. 11.—A "DEAD" DRAW, FOLLOW, OR MASSE IS GENERALLY BETTER THAN A "LIVE" ONE

THE truth of this principle is, of course, obvious. It is the old idea of staying near at least one ball and if possible near both. In nearly all massé shots one can stay near both.

Plate 102 shows the point. The massé shot illustrated is one frequently occurring in the "rail-nurse." The

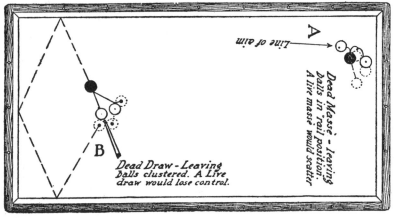

PLATE 102

draw position shown is one that often results in a perfect "line-nurse" position.

Particular need for the draw and massé to be "dead" occurs when the balls are in the open table, with no chance for the cushions or fortuitous "kisses" to help hold the balls.

125

CHAPTER XVI

PRINCIPLE No. 12.— ON OPEN TABLE SHOTS, IF NOTH-
ING BETTER OFFERS, TRY TO LEAVE AT LEAST ONE
BALL NEAR A CUSHION, AND IF POSSIBLE NEAR
A CORNER

POSSIBLY this hardly deserves to be ranked as a
"principle" of position play. It is more a matter
of "tight hole" tactics. But the situation arises so frequently that the idea is, nevertheless, well worth getting
firmly in mind.

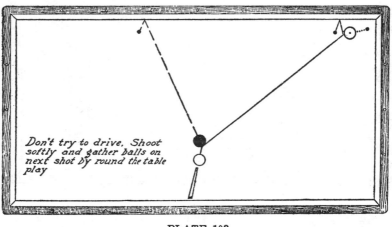

*Don't try to drive. Shoot
softly and gather balls on
next shot by round the table
play*

PLATE 103

Plate 103 shows a position where this is the point.
There are many. The first object ball cannot be well
driven around for a gather in the corner, either because
the cue ball is too near it, or because the cue ball could

126

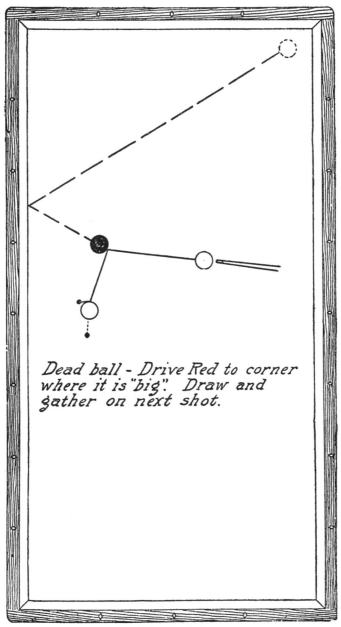

Dead ball - Drive Red to corner where it is "big". Draw and gather on next shot.

PLATE 104

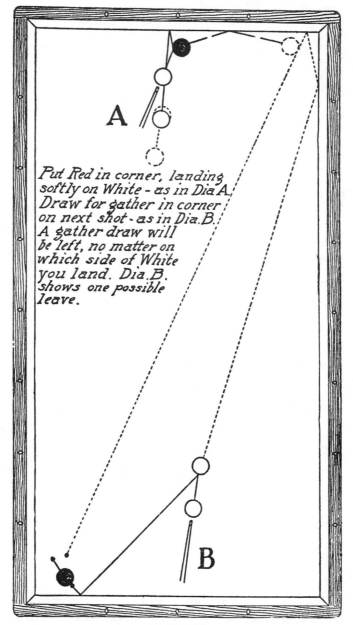

Put Red in corner, landing
softly on White - as in Dia A.
Draw for gather in corner
on next shot - as in Dia.B.
A gather draw will
be left, no matter on
which side of White
you land. Dia.B.
shows one possible
leave.

PLATE 105

not be made to land "dead" on the carom ball, or because a hard shot would jump the cue ball off the table. Shoot softly and there will be left a fairly easy round-the-table gather shot. Plate 104 shows another variation of this idea. Plate 105 shows still another. This one is played when the object ball (as in this diagram) does not lie favorably for it to be driven to the cushion and back to join the carom ball. If you land pretty fully on the carom ball, you are almost sure to get a draw for a gather, no matter which side of the carom ball you land on.

CHAPTER XVII

GETTING OUT OF HOLES — (A SEMI-ADVANCED POSITION PLAY) — A CONSIDERATION OF VARIOUS USEFUL SHOTS WHICH ARE OF GREAT HELP IN CERTAIN UNUSUAL POSITIONS

BEFORE taking up advanced position play, under which head we will consider "second ball play" and the various standard nurses, such as the "rail," the "line," the "anchor," the "chuck," the "rub," etc., let us consider some useful points in certain not infrequent but more or less difficult positions. Nearly all of them will be useful at times in primary as well as in advanced position play.

Some of these are little "tricks of the trade" that verge upon advanced work, but nearly all can be mastered by any fairly good amateur. The point lies not so much in the doing as the knowing of them.

Cue Ball English Transferred. — Plate 106 has to do with the effect of English transferred from the cue ball to the object ball. (See references to this on Plate No. 29.) Note particularly Diagrams A (the wrong way) and B (the right way). It is a simple little draw which every player meets time and time again. In making this shot it is very important to *draw to the inside edge* of the carom ball. Then, when the object ball comes back, it kisses the cue ball back and

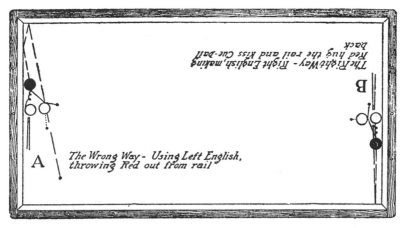

PLATE 106

itself stays nestled against the carom ball, offering the
" edge "-nurse, the " rail "-nurse, or some other form of
easy counting. This is a valuable shot, but it needs
patient practice, and in billiards patient practice pays
dividends in points.

Plate 107 is another illustration on the same point.

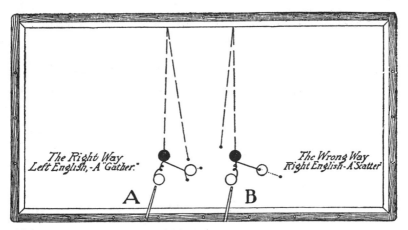

PLATE 107

How often it happens that your opponent closes his inning, leaving you a beautiful " set-up," out of which, much to your disgust, you make only two or three points before the balls are hopelessly out of position.

As a rule, the damage was done on the VERY FIRST SHOT. The leave was so easy! That is, the first point was. So you hastily blazed away, not stopping to notice that there were two, and perhaps three, ways to start off. You chose the most obvious, and it was the worst.

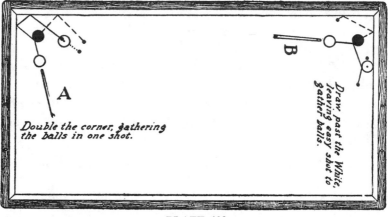

PLATE 108

Let us consider a few shots of just that character— " gay deceivers," they may be called. In Plate No. 108, Diagrams A and B: The obvious and simplest way is the easy " ball-to-ball " carom. But it will leave the balls spread and not " ahead " of you. Diagram A shows the way to gather them snugly by doubling the corner, instead of making the straight carom.

In B the player, instead of making the ordinary carom, draws softly past the edge of the carom ball for the first shot and gathers the balls on the other rail for the second shot.

I wish to call special attention to Plate No. 109, Diagram A. The picture shows the balls in mid-table, but the principle is the same anywhere, and most often this shot is played near the end rails. When you have a close draw, and the object ball is near the cushion, and will kiss back, it is of the utmost importance to *get the draw action* on your cue ball *quickly,* so that the cue ball is

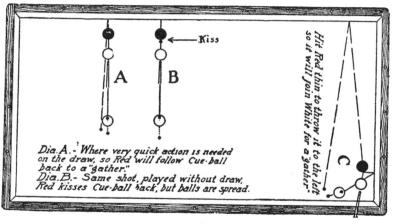

Dia. A.- Where very quick action is needed on the draw, so Red will follow Cue-ball back to a "gather."
Dia. B.- Same shot, played without draw, Red kisses Cue-ball back, but balls are spread.

Hit Red thin to throw it to the left so it will join White for a gather.

PLATE 109

well *under way* on its course back to the carom ball when the kiss takes place. Then, being under way, it *does not check* the object ball, which follows along with the cue ball to the carom ball, leaving all three together. If the cue ball is not under way, it will stop the object ball by its inertia when they kiss and leave the object ball standing where the kiss took place, the cue and carom balls on the other side of the table.

Sometimes to get the draw action on more quickly the

player may elevate the butt of the cue a trifle, giving the shot a little massé effect. If the cue and object balls are very close a full massé is used to get instant draw action.

For the shot shown in Diagram C hit the cue ball low and on the right, " swelling " back from the cushion.

In Plate 110, Diagram A, the important point is to hit the object ball full enough to bring it out to the carom

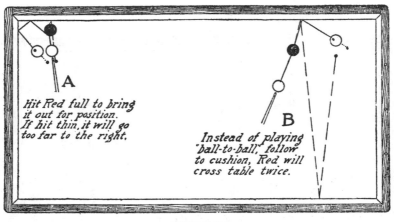

A

Hit Red full to bring it out for position. If hit thin, it will go too far to the right.

B

Instead of playing "ball-to-ball," follow to cushion, Red will cross table twice.

PLATE 110

ball, rather than to " cut it thin " and send it down the table. Hit the cue ball toward the top.

Diagram B shows a position where a ball-to-ball shot would spoil everything. By following to the cushion, driving object ball over and back again, landing dead with the cue ball, you can get a favorable position, where ordinarily a scatter looks more likely. Sometimes, on this, one can get the line-nurse on the second shot.

Plate 111, Diagram A, shows an easy way out of a line-up on the rail. By hitting the red ball full, with right English and follow, or " top," the red ball comes out from the rail, the cue ball follows in and caroms with the second ball on its return from the cushion.

B. *Massé Shot to hold Red ball.*

A

Top and right english and follow. The Red kisses out. Arrow shows where count occurs.

PLATE 111

Diagram B is drawn with an exaggerated curve, showing the course of the cue ball after a massé, so as to make the point of the shot clear.   In this position an

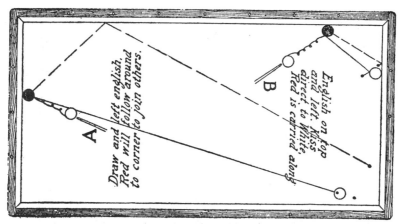

Draw and left english. Red will follow around to corner to join others.

A

B

English on top and left. Miss direct to White. Red is carried along

PLATE 112

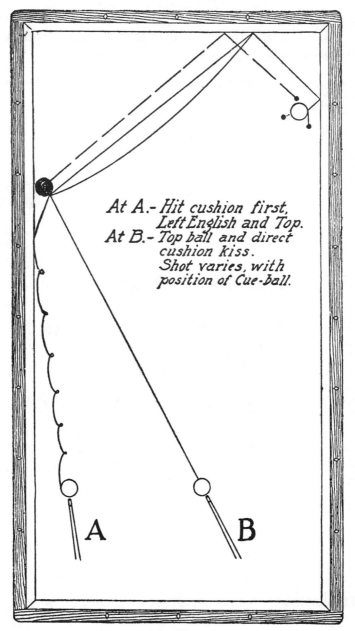

At A.- Hit cushion first,
     Left English and Top.
At B.- Top ball and direct
     cushion kiss.
     Shot varies, with
     position of Cue-Ball.

A   B

PLATE 113

ordinary massé or draw, hitting the object ball center, would drive it away. By the massé toward the right or mid-table side of the object ball you hold it back. This shot is rather difficult and requires practice.

In all these massé draws bear in mind what you want the object ball to do, as well as what you want the cue ball to do. If you want it to stay *on the same side* of the table, hold your cue *high.* Then the massé action takes effect quickly, and the object ball is hit lightly,

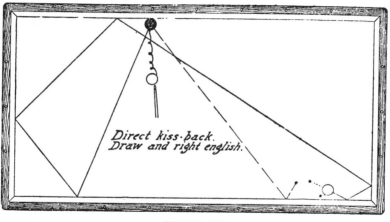

Direct kiss-back.
Draw and right english.

PLATE 114

leaving it behind. If you want the object ball to come back across the table *with the cue ball* to cluster with it and the carom ball, do not elevate the cue so much and go harder into the object ball.

In Plate 112 are two positions where the object ball is frozen to the cushion or very near it. In Diagram A, by drawing directly back from the object ball to the carom ball, one may not only count, but the object ball, forced into the cushion, "springs out" and will come to the

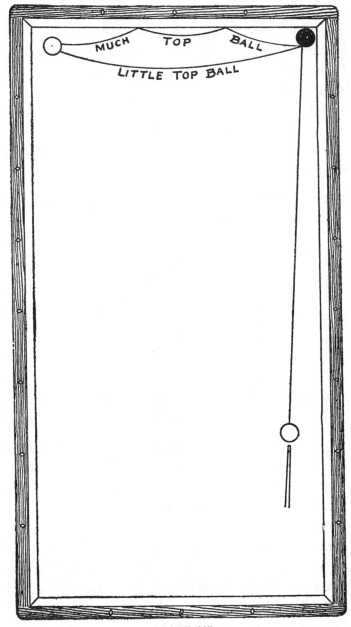

MUCH TOP BALL

LITTLE TOP BALL

PLATE 115

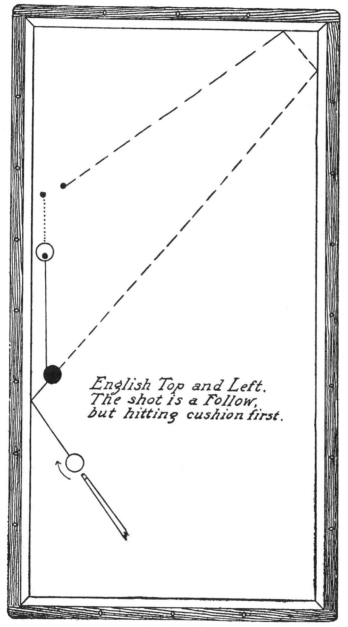

English Top and Left.
The shot is a Follow,
but hitting cushion first.

PLATE 116

corner with the others.   In Diagram B the same result is attained.

In Plate 113 the cue ball is shown in two positions, one near the left rail, the other in mid-table.   In the first case (A) hit the cushion first.   In the second (B) hit the ball first for a direct kiss.   In both cases the reverse English will deaden the cue ball on the end rail and all the balls will stop fairly close together.   The same shot may be made with the carom ball in the lower left-hand corner by giving the stroke a little more force.

Plate 114 shows a direct kiss back from the object ball, which is frozen to the side rail.   The cue ball is struck low, with reverse English.   The reverse becomes " direct " on contact with the *opposite* rail with the count easily effected, a fair position generally resulting.

In Plate 115 we show the two object balls in the extreme corners.   The principle of the shot is the same if they be closer together.   The cue ball must be hit high, and the object ball struck full as if for a follow. After the recoil from the contact the cue ball, still affected by the "top," seeks the end rail again, the degree of the curvature of its course, in the effort to get back to the rail, depending upon the force of the stroke and the amount of the follow effect.   The shot is impossible with " side " or draw English.

In Plate 116 is shown a position where the follow is impossible on account of a certain " kiss off."   The object ball is too close to the cushion for an inside shot with right-hand English.   But by using top and left English the cue ball will curve in toward the rail enough to count.

PART III

By Maurice Daly

Advanced Position Play

CHAPTER XVIII

SECOND BALL PLAY

THE dividing line between primary and advanced position play is not sharp. Some of the shots we have just considered might well be put under advanced work. The two divisions gradually and naturally merge into each other. But in advanced position play we may

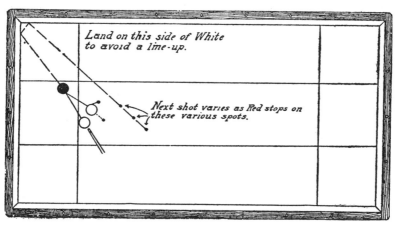

Land on this side of White to avoid a line-up.

Next shot varies as Red stops on these various spots.

PLATE 117

fairly count all that class of close work where "little differences make the biggest differences," where the utmost nicety of execution is required to give exactly the

143

right force, the right amount of English, and where, **by** perfect play, large runs may be made with the balls

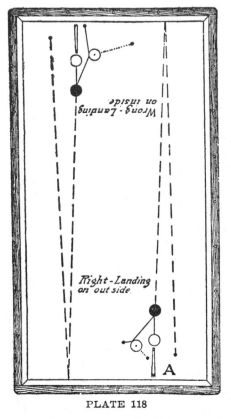

PLATE 118

moving but little and without driving around the table.

This is true "ball-to-ball" billiards and always has as a characteristic the point of LANDING ON THE SECOND BALL IN EXACTLY THE RIGHT SPOT, AND WITH THE RIGHT FORCE.

Therefore, in taking it up we will first consider some shots which will emphasize the principles of second ball play. This class of shots is not beyond any fair amateur, and a study of the principles cannot fail to enormously improve his game.

Where the cue ball lands on the carom ball is frequently of the most extreme importance. In close nursing the expert player will be seen taking the utmost pains at times, and to the tyro seemingly without necessity. The thing he is after is not only to make the count but in so doing to land on the carom ball in a particular spot to keep the balls "faced" right, or "under his hand."

Plate 117 shows a simple case of second ball play, an easy draw shot, the balls being as far at least toward mid-table, we will say, as the spot. The object here is to land on the "outside" ; i. e., the side near the other end of the table. Then the object balls will be toward the corners, and the player facing that way on the next shot.

A

Wrong, Landing inside.

Right, Landing outside.

B

PLATE 119

In Plate 118, Diagram A, is s h o w n a draw shot, say, of eight or ten inches. If the player d r a w s to the outside edge (left, as he stands) the balls will be left "ahead" of him and facing the corner, instead of leaving the cue ball between the other two. Sometimes, it is true, he wishes to land between them, to have a draw shot for the next, but in either case the point of the shot is *landing right* on the second ball.

Making his "land" properly, he has the balls still in control, with all kinds of possibilities, instead of a "saving-his-life" shot to make at any cost, regardless of position.

Plate 119 shows two of the easiest and most frequent examples of landing on the carom ball on the outside, leaving the balls in control, and facing the corner or end rail, with a choice of shots. Landing inside makes a long drive on the first or succeeding shots almost inevitable.

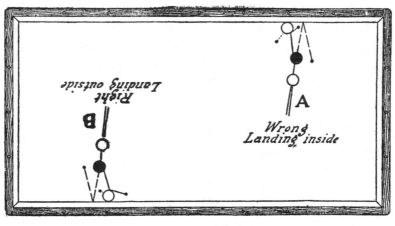

PLATE 120

Plate 120 shows another very frequent position, and these easy frequent cases are just the ones that will help you the most. So get them well in mind.

In Plate 121 is another common leave. The utmost care should be taken to land right on the second object ball. Hit the first object ball thin, shooting softly, and the resulting leave will be a simple draw shot that will leave the balls in the corner. If by hitting the first ball too full it then lands on the carom ball on the side near-

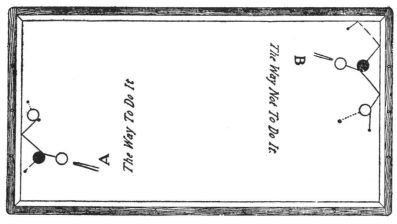

PLATE 121

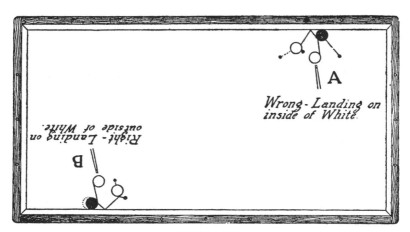

PLATE 122

est the rail, the result is almost sure to be a drive or some awkward shot, with possibly no chance to retain control.

When the two object balls are far apart on this shot it is not advisable to attempt too much, but when they are fairly close together it is always a place to attempt a correct landing.

Plate 122 shows the same idea on the side rail, but here the point is to gain, not a draw, but an easy carom or other close shot *without a long drive.*

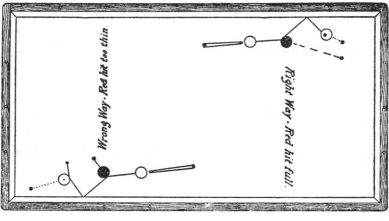

PLATE 123

Plate 123 explains itself. Here again landing right means control retained; landing wrong means a "saving-your-life shot."

Plate 124 shows a long follow down the side rail. At first glance one might say that the position shown was a parallel in billiard-principle to the short follows on the end rail. But the important difference is this — in the long follow you must hit the cue ball a pretty smart rap to follow so far; hence you are very unlikely to remain very near the second ball after the count and will force it toward the corner, leaving you some working space. The result is not nearly so likely to be favorable if your

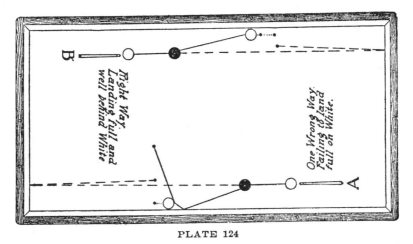

PLATE 124

cue ball lands either on the edge or on the cushion so far from the carom ball that it goes off the edge of the latter toward the center of the table.

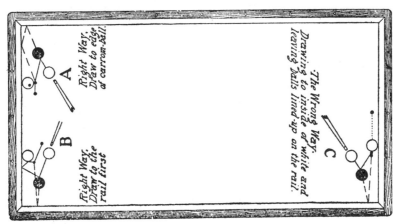

PLATE 125

If the follow be a short one, then some care must be taken so that the cue ball, after the count, may come out from the cushion and not leave a line-up. This may be done by landing with the cue ball on the cushion first, or by landing on the outside of the center of the second ball and kissing out.

In Plate 125 is shown a common and simple little draw shot. The result is shown if you draw to the edge of the

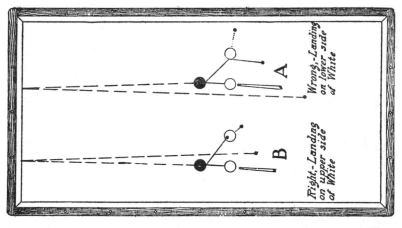

PLATE 126

second ball, leaving your cue ball out from the cushion and both object balls ahead of you. Another way of attaining the same result is shown in Diagram B — drawing to the cushion first and running out toward center of table. Each shot has its advantages and disadvantages. Method A is a little more exacting and therefore more likely to be missed. Method B may possibly leave your cue ball too far toward the center of the table to afford easy nursing thereafter.

Method C, however, admits of no argument. It leaves all three balls on the rail, and if not frozen, or very near it, the best you can get is a massé, or bank shot, or a scattering round the table shot.

Plate 126 shows a short draw shot, where the important point is to have the cue ball land on the far side of the carom ball. This will avoid a line-up and frequently the resulting leave will be an easy draw shot for the balk-line nurse. The leave may be a thin

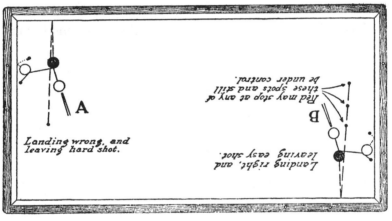

PLATE 127

shot, to be followed by a draw, or it may be a draw first, or even a follow, depending upon the original position of the balls (nearer or farther from the side rail you are facing while making the first shot), but in all cases you must *land on the second ball right.*

In Plate 127, again a short draw shot and drive, the object is to land behind the second ball, so that one ball, at least, is left "ahead" and facing a rail. The second shot may be a draw, thin shot, or half follow, but it *will not be a kiss-back*, which is always dangerous if of any length.

Plate 128 shows a position where lack of care will result in a "kiss-off" and too much force will give a "scatter" or a "line-up." Strike the cue ball above the center with reverse English, first object ball three-quarters full, carrying it along with the cue ball. The latter should strike the cushion almost directly behind carom ball to avoid a kiss; the "reverse" brings it up to the count, landing dead. This shot frequently gives the "line-nurse" position. The stroke should be made very easily.

Plate 129 shows the familiar "turning the corner" shot. Strike cue ball with left and top English, first object ball *full*, driving it around the corner to meet carom ball at the line. You will notice that this is a case of driving two balls, but *it is at close range*, where *control* is possible, and therefore admissible.

Practice this shot at various positions. You will then soon learn the slight differences which, in close work in straight rail billiards, give the "rail-nurse," or in balkline billiards the "line-nurse," or the "anchor" or "chuck-nurse" positions. You will see each time, what cannot be shown in a diagram very well, just where to land *on the second ball*, as well as how to bring the first ball around the corner. Generally you land dead as possible on the second ball.

Plate 130 shows a variation of this turning the corner, where you can land on the second ball "outside,"

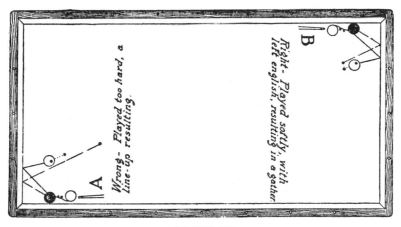

PLATE 128

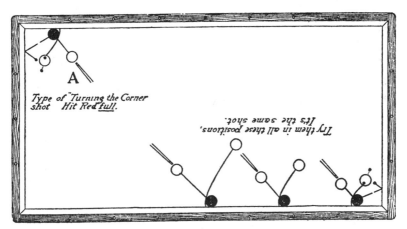

PLATE 129

just as easily as on the inside, and then get a better result, the balls facing the end rail.

In Plate 131 is shown one kind of a line-up that offers a perfect position shot. It is played as a follow. Cue ball catches the second object ball on the kiss. The shot must be made hard enough so that the kiss (which will stop the cue ball almost dead) will send the first ball over to the rail and back to the line for position. Wherever it stops it will probably be in a good position.

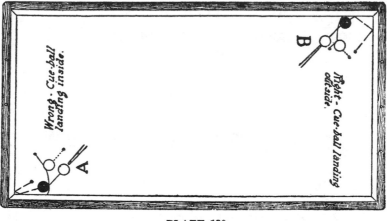

PLATE 130

Plate 132 shows the easiest way for a large class of shots where care must be used to keep cue ball "outside" (nearer mid-table after counting), so as to have more counts at command.

And here is an important point. This shot, in its variations, will frequently be such that the first object ball, on its return from the cushion may be made to *catch the cue ball on a kiss*, and will stop "dead" by the other ball.

The cue ball will not move far, and often the "anchor," "chuck," or "rail"-nurse positions will result.   As will be shown later, this is one of the shots experts use to attain one of these positions.

Plate 133 shows a case where the second object ball must be "loosened" from the cushion. If done exactly right, the cue ball may be left so that on the next shot all the balls may be brought t o g e t h e r

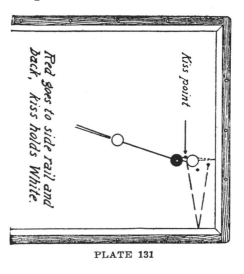

Red goes to side rail and back, kiss holds White.

Kiss point

PLATE 131

again.   Use *reverse* English on the cue ball, touching first object ball lightly so as not to drive it away.   Land

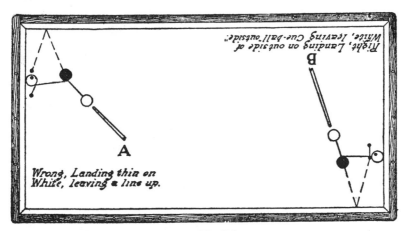

A

Wrong, Landing thin on White, leaving a line up.

B

Right, Landing on outside of White, leaving Cue-ball outside.

PLATE 132

pretty full on object ball so as to force it out to the side
rail and back, not frozen to either rail. This shot is
called for when second object ball is so near the far rail

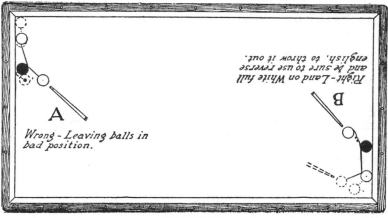

PLATE 133

that the cue and object balls are likely to nestle closely
together, leaving a difficult shot for a gather, even
though a massé might possibly make the count. If the

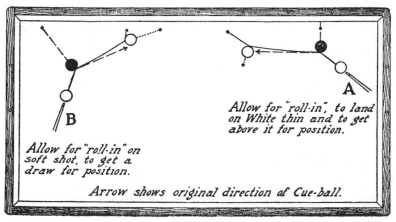

PLATE 134

second ball is not very near the far rail, the "draw-back," or "massé-back," position, already explained, may be used for the gather.

Sometimes it is desired to hit the second ball very thin, yet the cue ball has some little distance to travel from object ball to carom ball, and the shot must be made softly. In such cases, remember that on plain, slow caroms the cue ball, if true, will almost invariably *roll in* a trifle. So allow for it. Practice alone will tell you how much allowance to make for the "roll-in."

Plate 134 illustrates the point, one for a thin land, the other for a full land.

CHAPTER XIX

THE "CHUCK-NURSE"

A S a preliminary to the consideration of the standard nursing positions, the "chuck," the "rub," the "anchor," the "rail," and the "line," let us take a couple of diagrams illustrating again and impressing firmly a principle absolutely necessary in all of them. Then we will consider nursing positions in their natural order, "natural" in the sense that one leads to the other. And, also, they were developed, historically, in the order in which I have considered them.

Some exception may be taken to my placing the "anchor" before the "rail," but this is merely a matter of nomenclature. The word "anchor" was applied to this nurse after the balk-line game was invented. In the "anchor" the balls are astride the balk-line. But the shot was played before balk-lines were invented, though, of course, imperfectly, and for only small runs. Actually it originated as a part of straight rail work. Later, Jacob Schaefer discovered that he could work the same shot with the balls astride the line to defeat the balk. Then, and not till then, was it called the "anchor." Again, the "rail-nurse" is a *running*-nurse, and the anchor-nurse is a *stationary*-nurse. The running-nurse was of later development and grew out of the stationary.

In Plate 135 is shown a very important stroke, one absolutely necessary if you even aim to partly master the rail-nurse or the balk-line nurse. The point is as to the effect of English passing from the cue ball to the object ball. (See note to Plate 29.) If, in the shot shown, you English on the left, the object ball takes RIGHT English and MOVES TO THE RIGHT on the rail, keeping NEAR THE CAROM BALL. The other English would

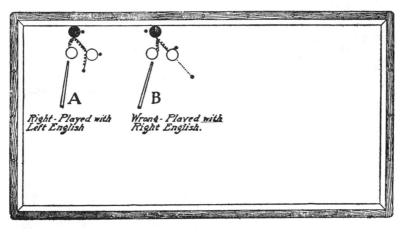

PLATE 135

leave the object ball standing still, instead of moving along to join its fellows.

This shot is the foundation of the rail-nurse and should be practiced with the balls at varying angles to get used to it — to see just how and how much the English takes. Try it with right English, then with left, and then with none. Master this and you have started on the rail-nurse, at which any good amateur should often run twenty-five or more, and at which some amateurs have made runs far into the hundreds.

The " Chuck-Nurse."—The principle just studied is important in the "chuck-nurse" when played in the balk-line game, for it enables you to keep the first object ball, frozen against the rail, from crossing the balk-line. The *"chuck"* position is shown in Plates 136 and 137.

In playing this shot do *not hit the cue ball below cen-*

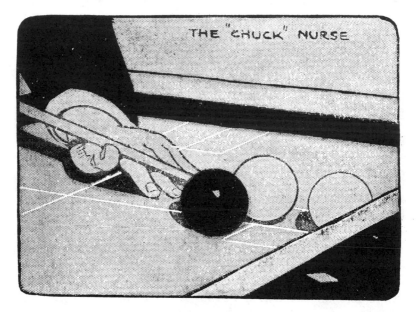

PLATE 136

Perspective view of the " Chuck-Nurse," at which W. A. Spinks ran 1010

ter. Hit it slightly *above*, and it slows up coming back for the count and lands softly. Hitting above the center also helps to keep the first object ball frozen to the cushion. You should try to have the cue ball land as NEAR THE EDGE of the carom ball as possible, and as softly as possible. The aim is to leave both object balls unmoved, so the carom may be repeated indefinitely. If in counting the cue ball freezes to the second object ball, so much the better. On the cue ball you may vary your English f r o m side to side as needed, to keep the first ob- ject ball in the same spot.

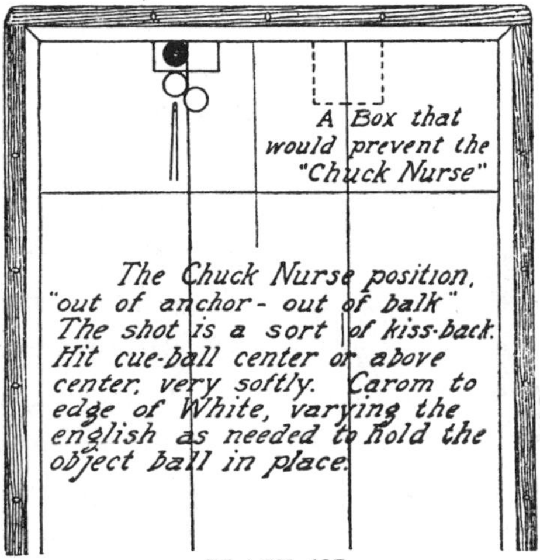

It is surprising how many points e v e n a fair amateur can make at this n u r s e if he plays softly enough and gets "the feel" of the stroke. You *j u s t t o u c h* the cue

A *Box that would prevent the "Chuck Nurse"*

The Chuck Nurse position, "out of anchor - out of balk." The shot is a sort of kiss-back. Hit cue-ball center or above center. very softly. Carom to edge of White, varying the english as needed to hold the object ball in place.

PLATE 137

ball, else the shot will be too hard. In Denver in 1912, Frank Dreiher, then an amateur, made a run of 245 at this nurse. William A. Spinks, now retired, but once a leading professional, made, in the fall of 1912, 1,010 points at this nurse in 18.2, and ceased play with the position still good. The plate shows the shot astride the balk-line, but the position is the same in straight rail, without balk-lines.

CHAPTER XX

THE "RUB-NURSE"

THE "rub-nurse" arose in the development of cushion caroms. It is the finest cushion carom position possible, sometimes resulting in very long runs. It is shown in Plate 138. In playing it the cue ball moves a small fraction of an inch and the object balls even less. I have seen Martin Mullen, an amateur, make more than 100 points at this nurse in cushion caroms, moving the balls only a few inches. It is just as useful in straight rail, and in balk-line astride the line at its end.

The cue ball strikes the cushion first generally (not always), with a little reverse English and "top." Then it caroms, but the reverse and top English deaden the cue ball so the object balls are scarcely disturbed.

Sometimes the chuck-nurse position grows out of spoiling the rubnurse position. But whenever you get the balls close

The Rub Nurse
Cue-ball top and reverse english. Cushion first, very softly, just barely getting to 2nd ball; then repeat.

PLATE 138

162

together on the rail, watch the chances to nudge them into one of these great positions, or into the anchor. The latter is far more difficult to execute, and in modern competition games it is barred as being too easy, though no players ever made many at it except Schaefer and Ives. In ordinary balk-line competitions I think by all means it ought to be allowed. It adds greatly to the variety of play and hence the interest of the game.

CHAPTER XXI

THE "ANCHOR-NURSE"

P LATE 139 shows the " anchor-nurse" position. It is shown with the balk-lines, but in straight rail billiards the position often occurs at other places along the rail. Many think that the anchor means the position where both object balls are frozen to the rail, side by side. But this, while a kind of anchor, is not the position made famous by Schaefer and Ives. In the real anchor one ball is frozen to the cushion, the other is out a bit. The ball on the rail is made to bear all the burden of impact of cue ball.

As shown in our plate the rail ball, on the first shot, is hit fairly full but very softly. The cue ball kisses off

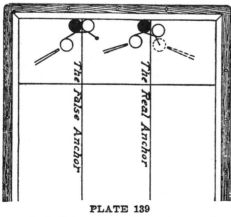

from this and just barely " grazes t h e glisten " of the second or free ball, and stops very near it. On the second shot the free ball is hit first, but it is barely grazed, *and not moved from its place.* The rail ball is met fuller, and the

PLATE 139

cue ball kisses up from it to the original position, just

where they were in the first place.

The anchor, it will be seen, consists of two shots, " going out and coming back," as the golfers would say. In this nurse, too, the effect of twist in holding the ball on the rail in place is important. But the nurse cannot be played except with the utmost delicacy, not to disturb the free ball from its position. After several shots it begins to settle into the cloth a bit, and as it settles it becomes " anchored " in its spot.

CHAPTER XXII

THE "RAIL-NURSE"

THE student, if he has practiced these shots, should now be ready for the rail-nurse. This is important, not so much for itself (in the larger cities little straight rail, unfortunately, now obtains among good players) as for the fact that it is the *best possible schooling for the balk-line nurse,* and indeed other position plays in countless number all over the table. Wherever close manipulation is called for there the principles learned in the rail-nurse come into play.

In my opinion, players take up the balk-line too quickly, and neglect the straight-rail game, to the detriment of their own play. Cushion caroms, too (not three-cushion caroms, however), is a game of the *very highest value* in its teaching effect, and of the utmost beauty in position-playing possibilities. For the competition player I cannot urge its practice too strongly in preparation for a match at balk-line.

First, in Plate 140, see illustrated the normal rail position, and a series of theoretically perfect shots. Ball No. 2 (on the outside) should travel along a straight line 4¾ inches from the rail. Ball No. 1 (on the inside) zigzags to and from the rail, and the two stop in a

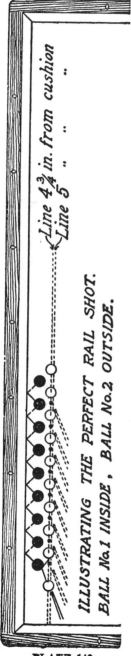

PLATE 140

Line 4¾ in. from cushion

Line 5

ILLUSTRATING THE PERFECT RAIL SHOT.
BALL No.1 INSIDE, BALL No.2 OUTSIDE.

duplicate of the original position each time, but a little bit further along the rail.

In all this discussion of the rail-nurse I refer to Ball No. 1, meaning the ball nearest the rail, and Ball No. 2, meaning the outside ball.

Perfect Execution Not Possible.— So much for the theory of the shot. Sometimes the player will make a series of these perfect shots. But even the most expert players make mistakes in execution. No. 1 (ball nearest rail) is hit too hard or too full or too easily. Sometimes ball No. 2 is forced outside of the five-inch line and it must be flocked back, or the nurse is lost, and so it goes.

The Rail-Nurse a Series of Mistakes.— The rail-nurse, therefore, as it comes into actual play, is for the most part a series of mistakes and shots to correct them.

In the normal, perfect shot very little English, generally none, is used, and the cue ball is hit center, or a trifle below. Some find that it aids delicacy in landing to elevate the cue butt a trifle and to hold the cue firmer in the cue hand.

Two Classes of Mistakes.— The

mistakes in execution may be divided roughly into two classes — first, mistakes which occur with both object balls still inside the five-inch line on completion of the count; second, those shots in which one or both balls get outside the five-inch line. In the next chapter we will take up the positions arising from the most frequent errors, with both balls left inside the five-inch line.

In making the normal shot, I must not forget to call particular attention to this: Ball No. 1 must not be left *on the cushion,* but it must come out to join ball No. 2. In so doing, however — and note this well! — *No. 1 must not be hit so hard as to make it kiss No. 2.* That would force No. 2 across the five-inch line.

Also, in making this carom the cue ball must land on the center or the veriest shade to the *outside* of center of ball No. 2. The beginner's tendency is to land on the inside of center, thus forcing ball No. 2 across the five-inch line and leaving his cue ball in between the two object balls.

In making the perfect or normal rail shot No. 2 ball moves from $2\frac{1}{2}$ to 3 inches; No. 1 ball, of course, by reason of its zigzag course, must travel a little farther. Therefore, it must get a trifle more impetus. You must land dead on No. 2, but not dead enough to freeze.

CHAPTER XXIII

THE RAIL-NURSE (Continued)

IN THE last chapter we saw in diagram how the theoretically perfect rail shot simply moved the balls along like a team of well-trained horses, ball No. 2 moving along in a straight path on an imaginary line about $4\frac{3}{4}$ inches from the rail, while ball No. 1 zigzagged in and out from the cushion, joining its mate and leaving a series of repetitions of the original position. Frequently the player will make a series of these perfect shots. But this twain of horses are trick horses. A mistake of execution comes and then the normal position has to be recovered by careful manipulation.

I have divided these mistakes into two classes, those that force ball No. 2 outside the five-inch line and those that leave it still inside the five-inch line.

In the diagrams shown herewith the balls are shown from positions occurring in actual play of the rail-nurse by myself, and they are drawn to exact scale.

In all this rail work the distance the balls travel on each shot is short, sometimes only a fraction of an inch, sometimes two or three inches, or in rare cases even as much as six inches, in certain recovery shots. Even repetitions of the "normal" shot are not perfect duplicates, and the minute differences, while not enough to destroy the position, may, nevertheless, make one shot in which the balls move half an inch and again two to three inches.

So great a difference does such a little difference make that it is impossible to do more by diagram than to show the principle. The player must practice the positions carefully and repeatedly, and learn by actual play just the "feel," amount of English, etc.

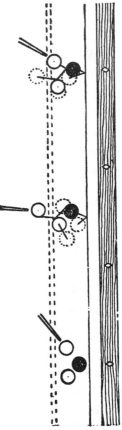

A.— Ball No. 1 did not go far enough to join No. 2. Cure — Cue ball "top" and left English, Ball No. 1 hit full, just enough off center to carom on right of center of Ball No. 2. It is a kiss shot from No. 1, and No. 1 "squeezes" along to the right.

B.— Next, fine shot, left English, landing on No. 1 quite full, to avoid line-up or freeze.

C.— Balls now in normal rail position again.
(Position No. 1 in each case is the result of faulty play with a perfect rail leave.)

PLATE 141

In the above illustration, as in similar ones further on, the first position shows the balls as they lie from an imperfect preceding stroke, and "out of position."

Key to These Particular Diagrams.— Note carefully : beside each position is printed a description of just how the shot is made to produce the succeeding position. In these shots the balls move along *very short distances.* The drawings separate the second position from the first, the third from the second, etc., a good bit to make it clear.

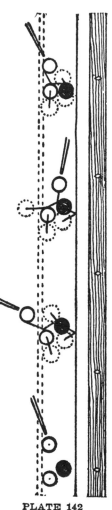

A.— Ball No. 1 was hit too hard as compared with No. 2 and got ahead of it. Cure—Hit No. 2 full, English on right to keep cue ball to right.

B.— Be sure now to have cue ball land to right of center of No. 2. Play easily, English right.

C.— Soft carom, English right; both balls move in toward the rail.

D.— The normal rail position recovered.

PLATE 142

In all these shots bear again in mind that you must not let ball No. 1 move so fast off the cushion as to kiss No. 2 out across the five-inch line. The two dotted lines are (on the plate) approximately 4¾ and 5 inches, respectively, from the rail, and along these lines the balls should be kept. *The prime dangers* as to this are that No. 1 stays too near the rail, and that No. 2 gets over the five-inch line.

CHAPTER XXIV

RECOVERY OF POSITION FROM OTHER FAULTY LEAVES
INSIDE THE FIVE-INCH LINE

A FAULTY position from playing the normal rail
shot is shown in Plate 143. Ball No. 2 (outside ball) was pushed a trifle too far to the left, because
the cue ball landed on it too far to the right of center.
Read the notes alongside the diagrams to see how to
regain the normal rail position.

One must always bear in mind in playing the rail or
balk-line nurses the fact that in driving an object ball
to the cushion *right English on the cue ball* gives the
object ball *left* English, and *vice versa.* Therefore,
when you want ball No. 1 to advance, in the rail position shown in these plates, left English helps it along
the rail and right English retards it.

The next faulty leave illustrated (Plate 144) sometimes arises from a lack of sufficient left English on the
preceding shot, thus failing to carry ball No. 1 (inside
ball) along ahead of the cue ball.

This position is one requiring extreme accuracy, especially on the first shot, which must not knock No. 2 ball
away.

At first you may have some difficulty in getting the exact amount of force in the shot. A little practice, however, will give the average player a surprising amount of control. In time the appreciation of just

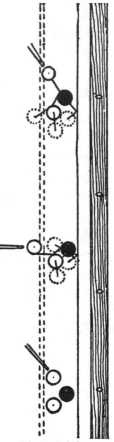

A.— First use plenty of left English, and hit No. 1 ball three-quarters full, a "half-follow" shot. This will "squeeze" No. 1 along the rail inside of No. 2 and push No. 2 out toward the five-inch line again.

B. —Now a very fine shot, with left English, to work No. 1 along toward No. 2. No. 1 kisses cue ball back to avoid a freeze.

C.— The result is the normal rail position again.

PLATE 143

how hard to hit the cue ball becomes subconscious. Practice on this will help you elsewhere in nursing. The great aid value to your general game that practice on this nurse gives, makes a little work on it desirable.

A.—In this case the cue ball got slightly ahead of Ball No. 1. Cure — Cue ball hit barely above center, with LEFT ENGLISH, kissing back and JUST GRAZING Ball No. 2, scarcely stirring it.

B.—A fine shot. Play very softly not to move No. 2. English left, landing on No. 1 full, but to the LEFT OF CENTER.

C.—Cue ball hit top and left, landing on No. 1, like a "half-follow" shot.

D.—Result, the normal rail position recovered.

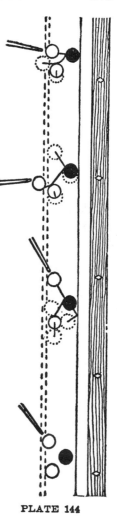

PLATE 144

CHAPTER XXV

RECOVERY OF POSITION FROM OTHER FAULTY LEAVES INSIDE THE FIVE-INCH LINE (Continued)

THIS chapter finishes the most important and common of the faulty leaves inside the five-inch line, made from the normal rail position as a start.

First, in this chapter take the case of the balls lying as shown in Plate 145, in which the cue ball got outside and possibly a bit ahead of ball No. 2. It is one of the shots that must be very exact in execution, and, if so, the desired recovery is effected in one stroke. This shot is difficult, the difficulty arising in getting enough follow

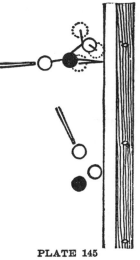

A.— A follow shot. English on the right to hold the object ball, which may even kiss off from carom ball a trifle. Cue ball lands fairly full on Ball No. 1, but on ITS LEFT HALF.

B.— The normal rail position regained.

PLATE 145

without hitting No. 2 too hard. Plate 146 explains itself.

176

A.— Ball No. 2 not far enough along. Very thin, just grazing Ball No. 1 (the white). Cue ball left English, going to cushion and coming out again 2 to 2½ inches.

B.— Result, the normal rail position regained.

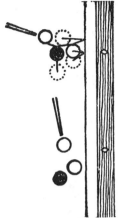

PLATE 146

There are also a number of mistakes made in the course of correcting mistakes, to regain the normal, but if you master the principles here illustrated the cures in these special cases will readily occur to you.

We next show a pair of massé positions, the result of which, in each case, if properly made, is the regaining of the normal rail position. (They are Plates 147 and 148.)

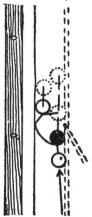

As the reader will suspect, the diagrams by no means exhaust the slightly differing faulty positions from which recoveries of the normal position may be recovered.

A.— A massé. Cue ball pushes No. 2 ahead, goes to cushion and lands very lightly on No. 1.

PLATE 147

But I illustrate the keynote shots. These mastered, you will see yourself the point of others that vary but little from them. You may even invent a shot or so.

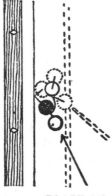

B.— Massé "squeeze," No. 2 ball being too far to the left. Cue ball lands full on No. 1 but on *the right of center* of No. 2 Ball. No. 1 "squeezes" in to the left of No. 2 and rushes it out. The normal rail shot regained, or nearly so.

PLATE 148

In the next chapter we will consider how to get ball No. 2 back, once it has crossed the five-inch line, which is the outer one of the two dotted lines shown in the plate. The 4¾-inch line is the one ball No. 2 should travel, with perfect shots.

Mentally Guiding the Shots. — In playing the normal rail shot (and, indeed, nearly all position shots) one must get into the habit of mentally guiding — for lack of a better term — the balls. Get the mental habit of seeing in your mind's eye the balls moving to certain positions. You see the very spots where you want the balls to stop, and you try to land them there. Mentally see them travel along their course to the fore-intentioned resting places and you'll find this habit of enormous assistance in making the balls do your mental bidding.

CHAPTER XXVI

RECOVERY OF POSITION WHEN THE OUTSIDE BALL GETS OVER THE FIVE-INCH LINE

WITH this chapter we close our examination of the rail-nurse, considering how to recover the normal rail position when ball No. 2 gets over the five-inch line, and considering how to "turn the corner" in order to go on with the rail-nurse, playing down the adjacent side rail or coming back on the same rail in the other direction. The practice of this nurse will be to the average player not only full of interest — for it requires perfect tools, a first-class table, and fine billiard technique — but it will be of immense value in the study of balk-line. It is, in fact, practically an *absolute necessity* to the mastery of line work. There is no other nursing practice for the average player so good as practice on the rail, so good for the cultivation of a nice sense of touch, that sub-conscious mastery of muscles that enables one to drive the ball just so far as desired. The game is full of niceties that give billiards its chief charm, and, as a matter of fact, it is harder for the average amateur to play straight rail *up to its possibilities* than it is in balk-line.

In Plate 149 we show ball No. 2 part way over the five-inch line. Now, *get this firmly in mind:* When

No. 2 ball starts breaking away to the right, *go after it at once.* And the general plan is to get either a carom or a " kiss back " which will leave the cue ball *to the right of* No. 2 ball. Then the next shot, by hitting No. 2 as full as the position allows (on right of No. 2's center), will edge No. 2 back to the five-inch line. But the *first* step, you see, is to get the cue ball

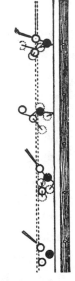

A.— The "kiss-out" shot. Hit No. 1 full, with slight draw. No. 1 goes to cushion, comes back and "kicks" cue ball over the five-inch line, cue ball JUST GRAZING No. 2. No. 1 Ball, after the kiss, joins No. 2 without knocking it away.

B.— Hit No. 2 to right of center, driving 1 to 1½ inches. No. 2 Ball will then cross inside of the five-inch line.

C.— Hit No. 1 full. It cushions, "kicks" cue ball and joins No. 2 in the normal rail position again.

D.— The normal rail shot regained.

PLATE 149

TO THE RIGHT of No. 2; that is, well outside the five-inch line, generally as much as two inches.

With this plate (No. 149) a position in which No. 2 was forced over the line by No. 1, the latter coming out from the cushion too strong, will be found directions for the recovery of rail position, starting with the so-called " double-kiss " out, though in reality only one " kiss " occurs.

Sometimes, if both balls get well out from the cushion, with No. 2 just over the five-inch line, a simple carom shot, with cue ball landing on right of center of No. 2, will put the balls in position for the "recovery shot" as shown in the position C on Plate 149.

If the "kiss-out" is needed, there's one thing to practice and remember. If one ball is directly out from No. 1 (which is near the cushion), use *left English*. If only slightly to the left of No. 1, *use no English*. If still a trifle more to the left of No. 1, *use right English*, in order that No. 1 may not advance too far.

CHAPTER XXVII

" TURNING THE CORNER " SHOTS

PLATES 150, 151, and 152 show three ways of "turning the corner," the object being to get the balls either on the next rail in normal rail position for a

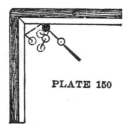

PLATE 150

Top and left, like "half-follow" shot. Cue ball going to cushion. Sometimes you simply kiss back from No. 1 to No. 2, using right English to throw No. 1 Ball around the corner. Resulting normal rail position (on the other rail) shown by small figures.

PLATE 151

Thin on No. 1, full on No. 2. Resulting normal rail position shown by small figures (headed in the other direction).

PLATE 152

No. 1 hit full (left English), cue ball following to left EDGE of No. 2. Dotted outline figures show new rail position on other rail.

182

continued rail-nurse, or to *turn back* along the same rail, faced in the opposite direction from that in which you have been nursing them.

There are various modifications of these, and one or two massé "turns," but get these in mind and others will become obvious to you without difficulty.

CHAPTER XXVIII

"RAIL-NURSE" PRINCIPLES APPLY TO THE "BALK-LINE" NURSE

WE WILL consider now simply the balk-line nurse, which will be found to contain little really new to one who has learned the rail-nurse well. It is the rail-nurse at longer range. And as the balk-line is 18 inches from the rail, it requires higher exactness for perfect execution, with much less opportunity for the recovery of the normal " line " position after a mistake.

First, in Plate 153, we see the balls (Positions No. 1, No. 2, and No. 3) in position where by driving No. 1 to the cushion it can be made to rejoin No. 2 and leave the cue ball in position for some soft caroms. The important point to consider here is the angle A-B.

In Position No. 1 use *right English* and draw softly to center (as you face No. 2, not to center on the long rail).

In Position No. 2 use *no English* and draw as before.

In Position No. 3 *use left English* and draw to " throw " object ball (No. 1) to the right, to join No. 2.

Bear in mind in judging just what point you wish to bring the object ball back to *that the second object ball will naturally be moved to the right* a trifle on making of the count by the cue ball.

Another thing that lends perfection to the execution of this shot is this: While hitting object ball No. 1 hard enough to bring it back near the others it is far *better to hit it only just hard enough to bring it back to them,*

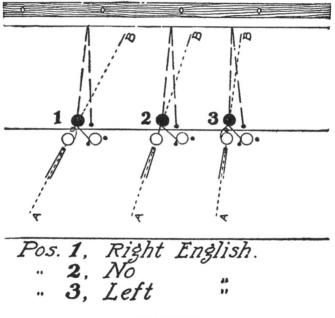

Pos. 1, Right English.
" 2, No
" 3, Left "

PLATE 153

Dotted line A-B shows varying angle toward cushion that cue ball takes. The angle is the real difference in positions 1, 2 and 3.

but not to kiss them hard, and especially—VERY IMPORTANT!—*not to kiss object ball No. 2 away.*

A kiss on the cue ball may not harm if full in center, but if the kiss is not in the center or *very near* it, or if the object ball comes back too swiftly, it will break up the position. This is just as in the rail-nurse, No. 1

ball must not come out so fast as to kiss No. 2 across the five-inch line.

The drive in-and-out from the cushion is the *keynote of the balk-line nurse,* for one will not easily miss the soft caroms which come in between the drives in and out from the rail. The important shot to make perfectly is the drive shot, and it is, therefore, important, in making the soft caroms, to so make them that the drive shot shall be direct and easy, instead of at an angle, when English will be needed to correct the come-back angle.

The point about *not* bringing the driven ball back *too rapidly* is very important. In this one thing lies the difference between the modern way of playing the line-nurse and the old way. Formerly it was the practice to play for the kiss between the object ball No. 1 and the cue ball on the return. But the best players nowadays do not play for the "kiss-and-stop" EXCEPT WHEN THE "KISS-BACK" IS PERFECTLY STRAIGHT (or nearly so) or when object ball is a wee bit too far to the left to be in the perfect position for the drive in and out.

If the object ball, coming back from the cushion, only *just gets to* the others, there is much *more leeway for error* in its stopping point (as to right-ness or left-ness as you face it on the come-back). A variation of nearly three inches may occur with the balls still left so that on the next drive in and out you can retain control.

First get this "drive in-and-out" shot well practiced, so that you can properly guide the object ball to right or left with changing English and bring it back just far enough, and not too far, so as to kick the others away. Then take up the next diagrams.

A.— The pure balk-line nurse position. Here the first thing to do is to make one, two, or even three or four, soft caroms to get the balls in the second position.

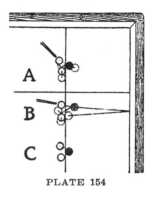

B.— In this second position the leave may not be perfect. It may vary in an angle to the cushion, as shown in Plate 153, and when you drive Ball No. 1 to the cushion, varying English may be required to bring the ball back to the point required, as previously explained.

PLATE 154

C.— But supposing you have executed the " drive-in-and-out " perfectly, the balls are now on the line again, ready for some more soft caroms, preparatory to another drive in-and-out, and so on ad infinitum.

Ball No. 2 must always be kept outside of the balk-line. Then the balls are " out of balk," and can be manœuvered with the line-nurse so long as you are able to execute it.

Sometimes the two will separate, or the cue ball will get too far ahead of No. 1 (to its right), so that the proper plan will then be to " slip through " No. 1 and No. 2, and then play the line-nurse, driving to the other cushion. Sometimes by use of the " edge-nurse " (passing back and forth across the face of the two object balls, just grazing them) they may be coaxed back into the line-nurse position. But for these various forms of close manipulation we will refer to the later chapter devoted exclusively to " close manipulation." But the things learned in " recovery of rail position from faulty leaves " will also be of help in recovery of line positions from faulty strokes.

CHAPTER XXIX

"TURNING BACK" WITH THE LINE NURSE

IF THE balk-line nurse position be attained in the "short table," play it as long as you can hold the balls in that position. If it be attained above the cross-table balk-line, but somewhere near it, and you are working with it down the table ("facing the open sea"), it is generally wiser to "turn the balls" and by the "going-through" shot to head toward the end rails again and work toward the short table, still retaining the line position by this manoeuvre. Now, when the balls begin to act badly, as they are *certain to do sooner or later*, you will be in a part of the table where there are *many ways* to retain control.

The way to handle this "turning around" is by the "slip-through" shot, shown in Plate 155.

In this plate the balls are shown well apart, to make the tactics clear. In actual play one should keep them as close together as possible, and move them as little as possible, only fractions of inches.

First you hit the ball *nearest the side rail* a wee bit fuller than the other, shooting very softly. In all soft nursing it aids to soften the contact of cue ball with object ball to hit it *below center*. Some also hold that it is of assistance to this same end to grip the cue firmer.

189

This is probably, however, a case of the personal equation.

By hitting the inside ball a bit fuller you *edge it down table* beyond the other. One or two of these preparatory shots and the balls open up a bit so you can slip through. That leaves you with the line position still, but you are now headed *the other way*, toward the short table again. The possibility of the same tactics often arises in other places, and in straight rail. The slip-through shot is of wide and valuable use.

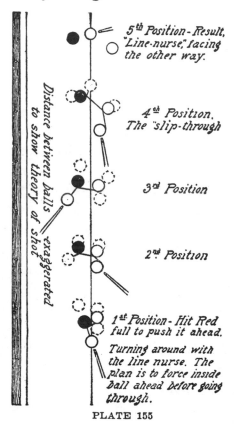

5th *Position - Result, "Line-nurse," facing the other way.*

4th *Position. The "slip-through"*

3rd *Position*

2nd *Position*

1st *Position - Hit Red full to push it ahead.*

Turning around with the line nurse. The plan is to force inside ball ahead before going through.

Distance between balls to show theory of shot exaggerated

PLATE 155

Some of the finest players do not let the balls, when working along the line, get so far from the end rail as the spot, but slip through and turn back at about the cross-table balk-line or not far below. I believe thoroughly in these tactics. It is around here that the nearby cushions offer favoring angles for cushion drives, once the balls begin to act badly. The same position *that in mid-table would be very bad* may, near the end rails, offer *no difficulty whatever.*

This is particularly true of massé-shot leaves. Mid-table massé shots are always dangerous, on account of the long reach required. I consider positions near the end rails fully 100 per cent more advantageous than even the best positions in mid-table, and always figure to get back to the end rails *at once.* With even first-class players no mistake of judgment is so common as sticking too long to mid-table nurses, without turning back, unless it be the sin of driving two balls.

CHAPTER XXX

GETTING "THE LINE" FROM CERTAIN FREQUENT LEAVES

IN BALK-LINE billiards the line position is always highly desirable, though whether the most desirable may be a question, depending upon the player's individual abilities and personal liking. With Schaefer and Ives the "anchor" (before it was barred) was the position most sought. The "chuck-nurse," in my opinion, is an especially desirable position if at that balk-line contact point where the reach is not bad and the play is right-handed for a right-handed player. In 18.1 it is particularly valuable, though in that form of billiards difficult to get. In 18.2, having a preparatory shot allowed in balk, it is much easier to get, and just as remunerative when attained. Always keep it in mind whenever the two balls are close together near the "contact points," i. e., where the long balk-lines meet the end rails.

W. A. Spinks, in practice, has made 1,010 at it, and some of these days I expect to see some professional make a very long run in competition. It is always good for a collection of easy points, and when it breaks up the balls are still in control. In playing it, however, the arm soon tires, which does not happen with the anchor, the line or the rail nurses, yet it is an infinitely easier nurse to play for a while than the anchor.

It is difficult to know where to begin, so many are the cases in point. We will examine some of them, and, with these learned, the student will see more himself. I see new ones almost every day, so infinite in variety is billiards.

Let us first consider some of the more obvious cases — where the balls may be put into *the line position in one shot*, as in Plate 156. Diagram A shows a follow shot.

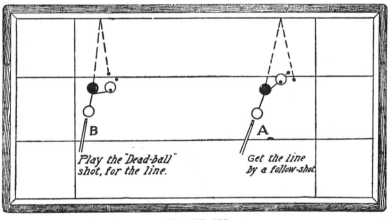

B
Play the "Dead-ball" shot, for the line.

A
Get the line by a follow-shot

PLATE 156

Hit ball No. 1 three-quarters to seven-eighths full, land on No. 2 slightly above (to left) of center. Slow follow.

Diagram B, a " dead-ball " shot. The danger here is that you *will not hit the first ball full enough*, and then land too hard on No. 2, knocking it away, or not " blocking." If you do not " block," ball No. 1, if hit even a wee bit too hard, will slip through the opening between cue ball and No. 2 and be lost.

A series of plates follow. The lettering on each plate tells the story in each case sufficiently well.

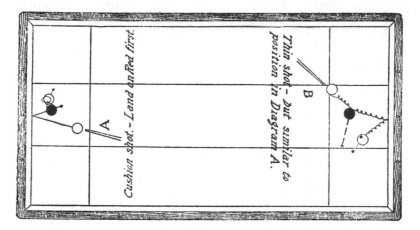

PLATE 157

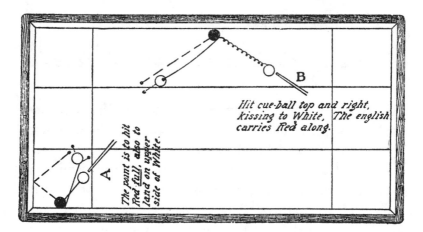

PLATE 158

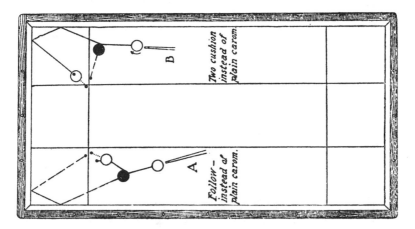

PLATE 159

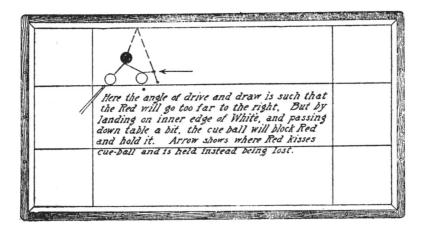

PLATE 160

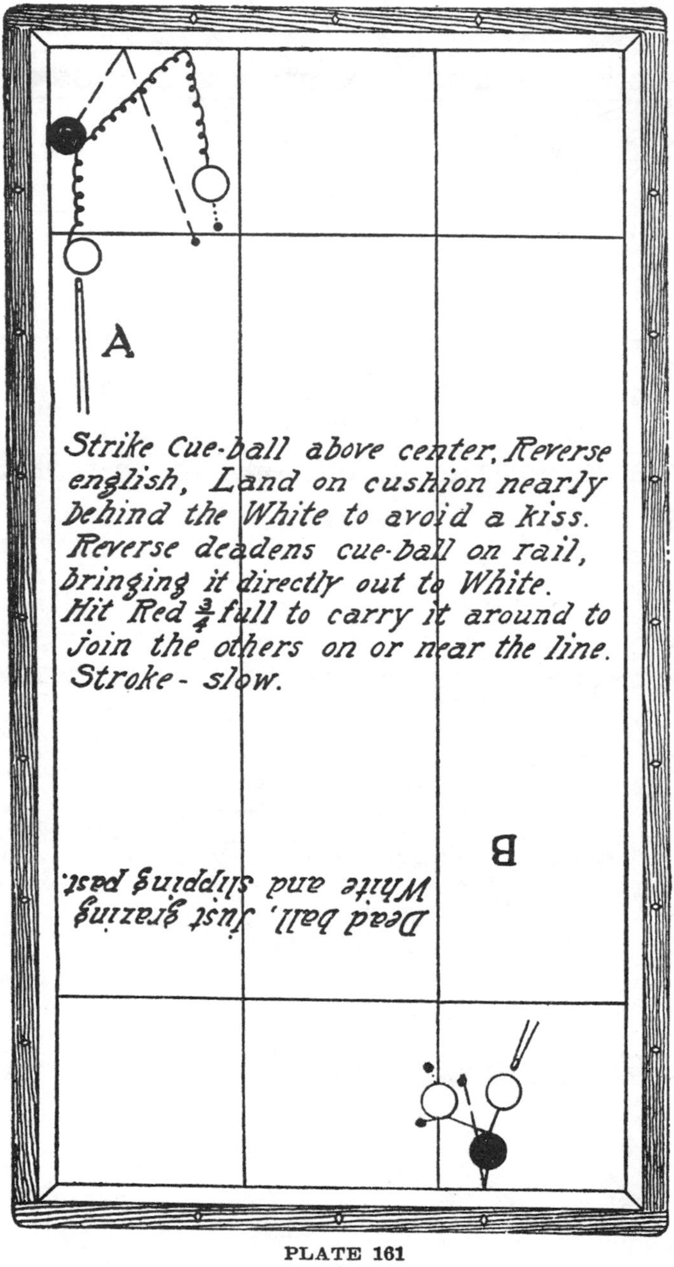

A

Strike Cue-ball above center. Reverse
english. Land on cushion nearly
behind the White to avoid a kiss.
Reverse deadens cue-ball on rail,
bringing it directly out to White.
Hit Red $\frac{3}{4}$ full to carry it around to
join the others on or near the line.
Stroke - slow.

B

Dead ball, just grazing
White and slipping past.

PLATE 161

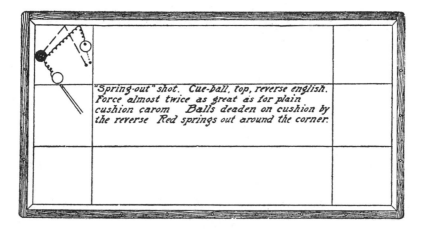

"Spring-out" shot. Cue-ball, top, reverse english. Force almost twice as great as for plain cushion carom Balls deaden on cushion by the reverse Red springs out around the corner.

PLATE 162

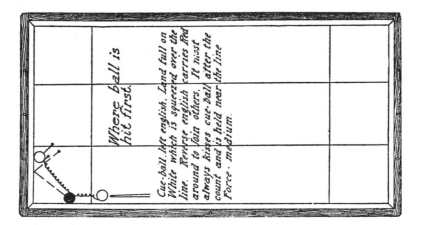

Where ball is hit first.

Cue-ball, left english. Land full on White which is squeezed over the line. Reverse english carries Red around to join others. It most always kisses cue-ball after the count and is held near the line Force · medium.

PLATE 163

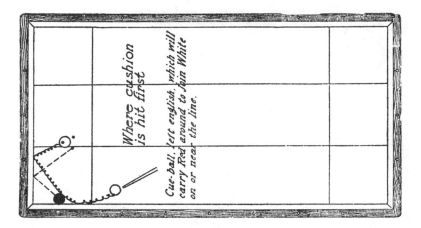

PLATE 164

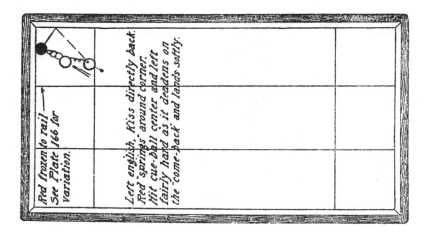

PLATE 165

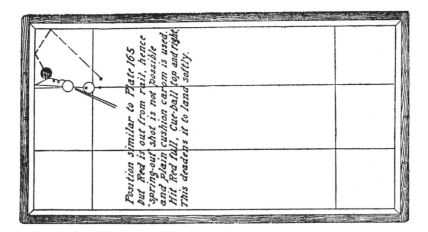

PLATE 166

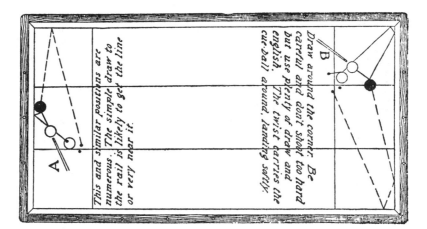

PLATE 167

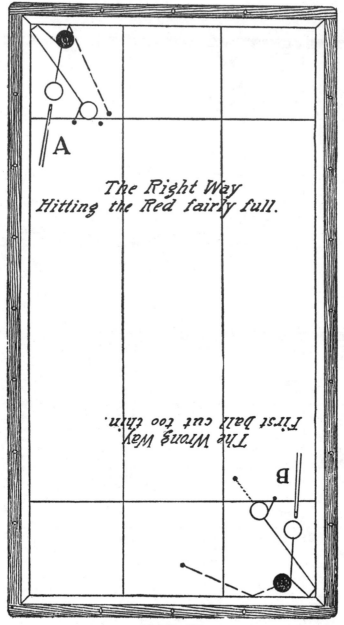

PLATE 168

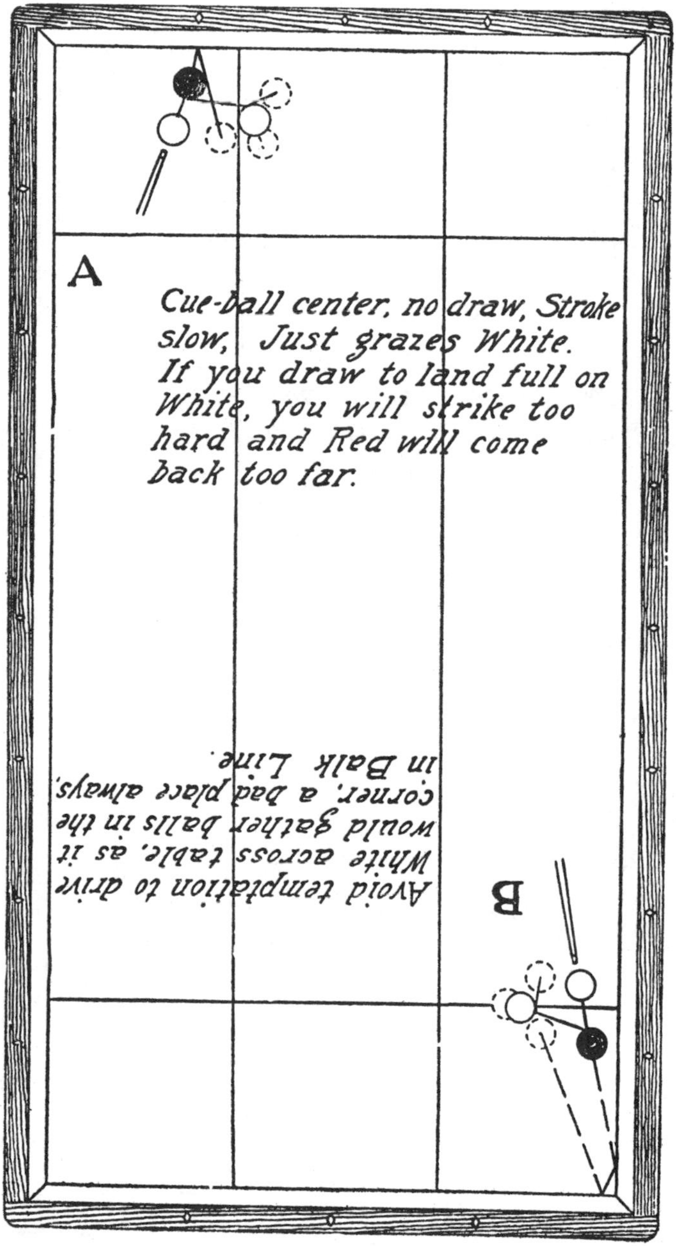

A

Cue-ball center, no draw, Strake
slow, Just grazes White.
If you draw to land full on
White, you will strike too
hard and Red will come
back too far.

B

Avoid temptation to drive
White across table, as it
would gather balls in the
corner, a bad place always,
in Balk Line.

PLATE 169

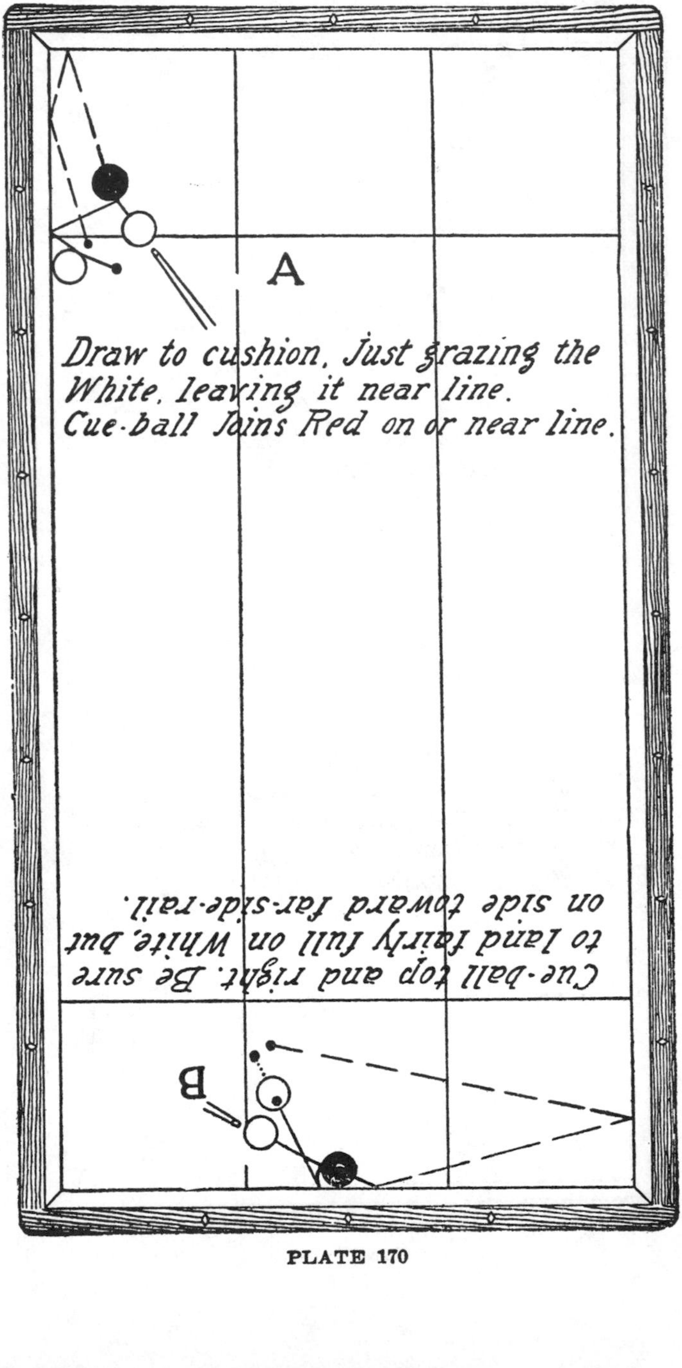

A

Draw to cushion. Just grazing the White, leaving it near line. Cue-ball Joins Red on or near line.

B

Cue-ball top and right. Be sure to land fairly full on White, but on side toward far-side-rail.

PLATE 170

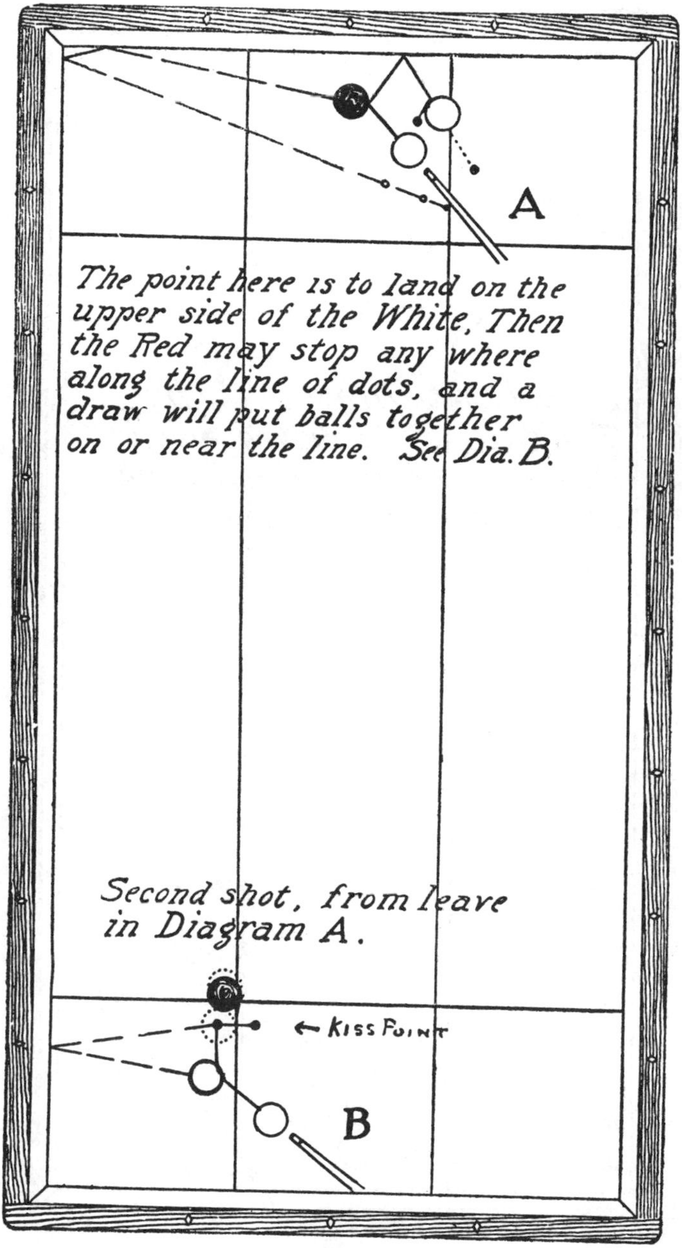

The point here is to land on the upper side of the White, Then the Red may stop any where along the line of dots, and a draw will put balls together on or near the line. See Dia. B.

A

Second shot, from leave in Diagram A.

← KISS POINT

B

PLATE 171

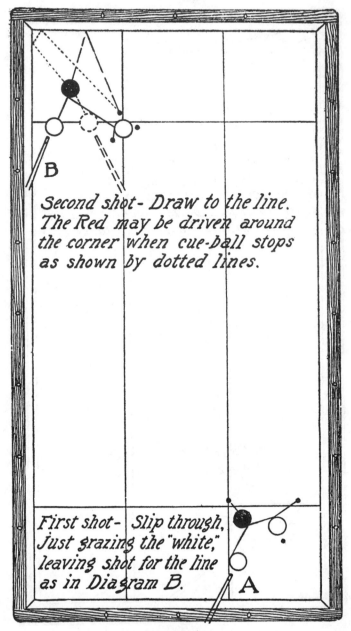

Second shot - Draw to the line.
The Red may be driven around
the corner when cue-ball stops
as shown by dotted lines.

First shot - Slip through,
Just grazing the "white,"
leaving shot for the line
as in Diagram B.

PLATE 172

Getting the Line in Two Shots.— The diagrams (172 to 175) alone will tell most of the story here. Bear this in mind: learn to recognize at a glance these familiar positions from which a good chance to get the line or near it in one shot is possible. Then other positions will be noticed where the first shot may be made to put the balls in one of these familiar positions which you know

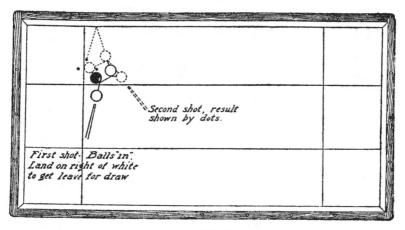

Second shot, result shown by dots.

First shot- Balls in. Land on right of white to get leav for draw

PLATE 173

as "line positions in one shot." Thus you come to know which are "line positions in two." Some of the more obvious and frequent ones are given in diagram.

Getting the Line in Three Shots.— Getting the line in three or more shots is generally a matter of manipulating the balls when they are already somewhere near the lines and under control. One of the most useful shots to know of this variety is shown in Plate 176, where the two object balls are side by side or nearly so and the cue ball near enough so that a very slow shot will not roll off.

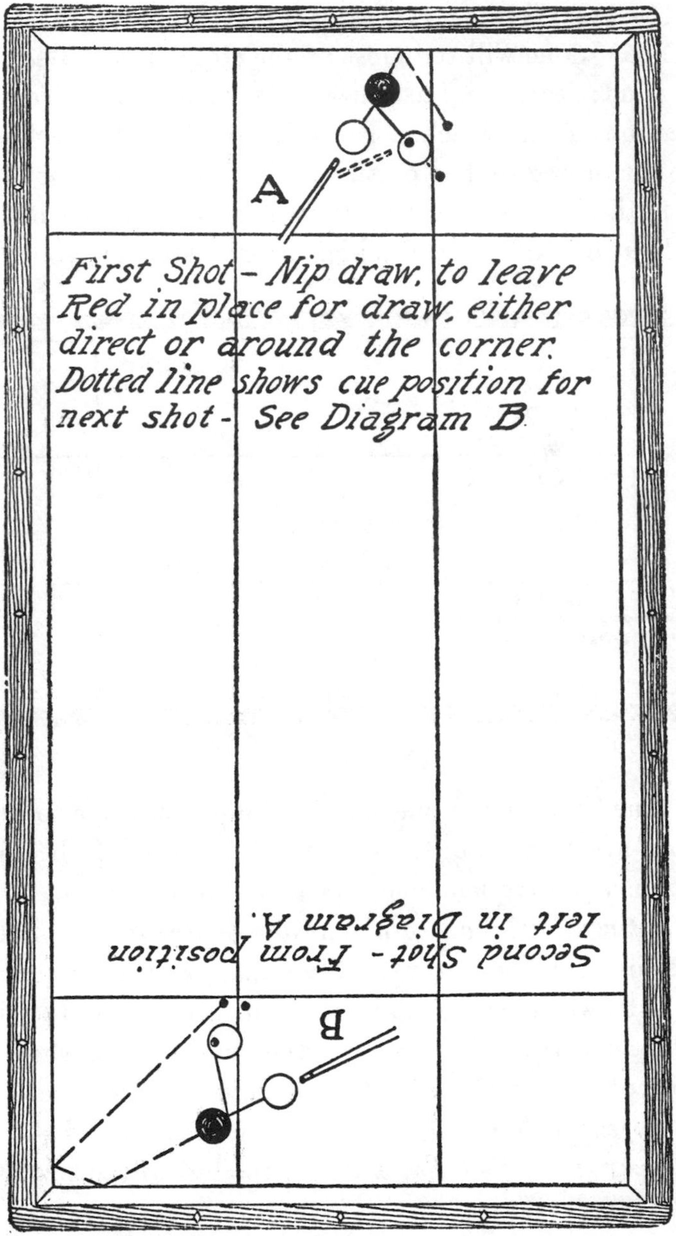

A

First Shot – Nip draw, to leave
Red in place for draw, either
direct or around the corner.
Dotted line shows cue position for
next shot – See Diagram B.

Second Shot – From position
left in Diagram A.

B

PLATE 174

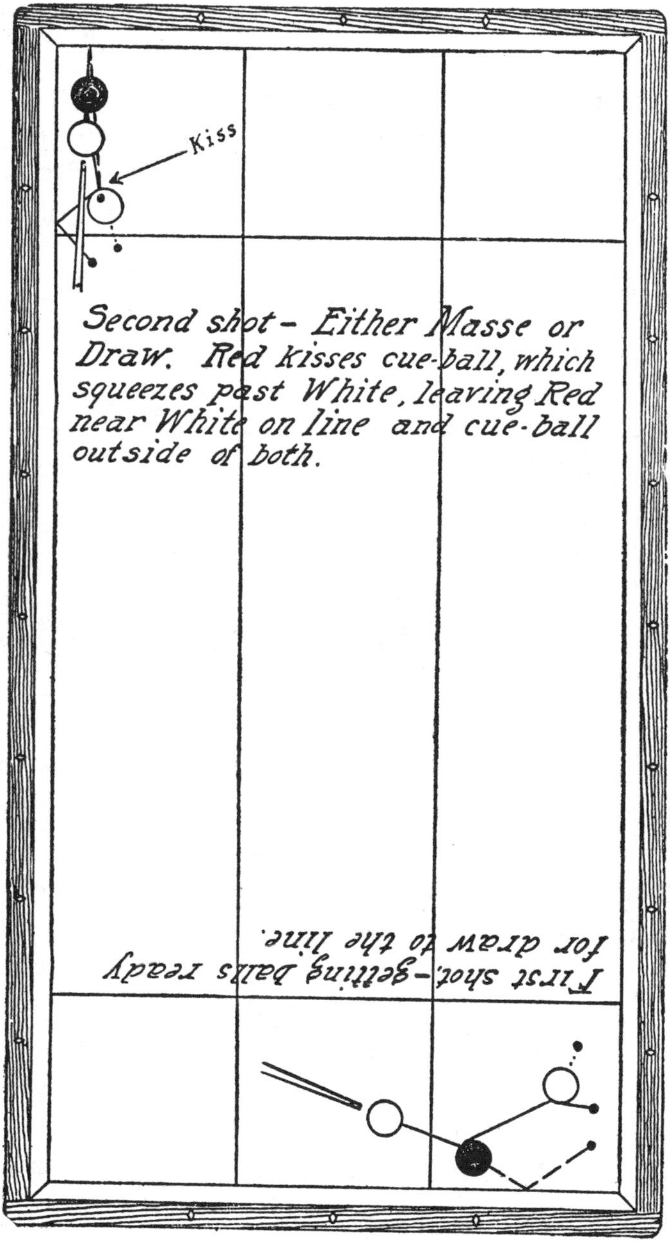

Kiss

Second shot – Either Masse or
Draw. Red kisses cue-ball, which
squeezes past White, leaving Red
near White on line and cue-ball
outside of both.

First shot – getting balls ready
for draw to the line.

PLATE 175

The important point is the *very first shot*. It must be not too hard, nor yet too soft. The first object ball should move forward generally about two inches, not more than three, as a rule. This will depend a bit on just how the balls face you on the first shot. The object of the first shot is to push No. 1 ball ahead

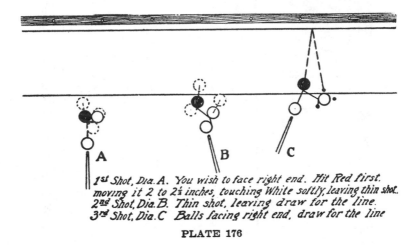

1st Shot, Dia. A. You wish to face right end. Hit Red first. moving it 2 to 2½ inches, touching White softly, leaving thin shot. 2nd Shot, Dia. B. Thin shot, leaving draw for the line. 3rd Shot, Dia. C Balls facing right end, draw for the line

PLATE 176

a bit and leave " the thin shot" for the second, enabling you to land on the second ball just where you need to get a draw and gather for the line.

This shot is useful in a great many other places, as well as in getting the line.

Now, notice in this situation you may choose which way of the table you wish the balls to face after the two shots are completed. If you wish to face the *right*, shoot on the *left* ball, *first* shot. And if you wish to face the *left*, shoot on the *right* ball first shot.

In Plate 177 the balls are shown astride the line, facing the side rail, and in position for the soft " edge-

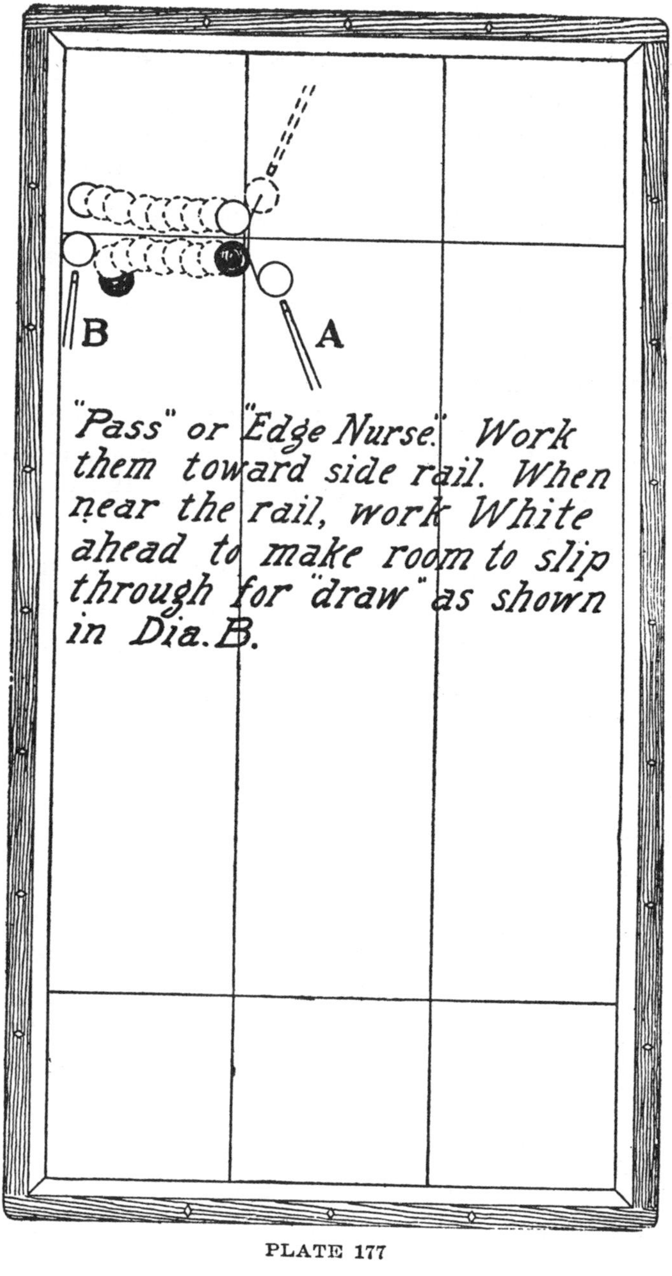

"Pass" or "Edge Nurse." Work them toward side rail. When near the rail, work White ahead to make room to slip through for "draw" as shown in Dia. B.

PLATE 177

nurse." The dotted lines show the successive positions of the two object balls as you pass across the face of the two with the " edge-nurse."

NOTE CAREFULLY: When they have been gotten near the rail, *but not till then,* by hitting ball No. 2 (on the right) a shade harder than No. 1 you work it along faster. You can then " slip through," leaving an easy draw for the line-nurse position.

As a general practice, whenever the balls are well set for the edge-nurse use it at once for as many as you can get out of it. They are the cheapest points you can find.

The " getting-the-line " scheme outlined above can be worked at any of the eight places where the balk-lines go to the rails.

CHAPTER XXXI

GETTING "THE RAIL-NURSE" POSITION

IT WOULD be an endless task to illustrate all the possible ways of getting the "rail." In the old days, when the experts played it, it was almost a sure thing that once the balls were well in the short table the player would have them "railed" in at most half a dozen shots. But a few examples will give a helpful notion of some of the more important position plays to "get the rail."

Getting the rail.

Kiss off the Red, Reverse english, Stroke easy. Red springs around and Joins White

PLATE 178

The diagrams 178 to 186, inclusive, will need no explanatory text.

On plate 179 the three succeeding positions, as drawn, are widely separated on the table. In actual play the balls move very, very little. But to draw the succeeding positions close together, would not result in clearness. The balls remain at the same place on the rail all during the "loosening" process. Then on resuming the rail-nurse they work along slightly with succeeding shots.

211

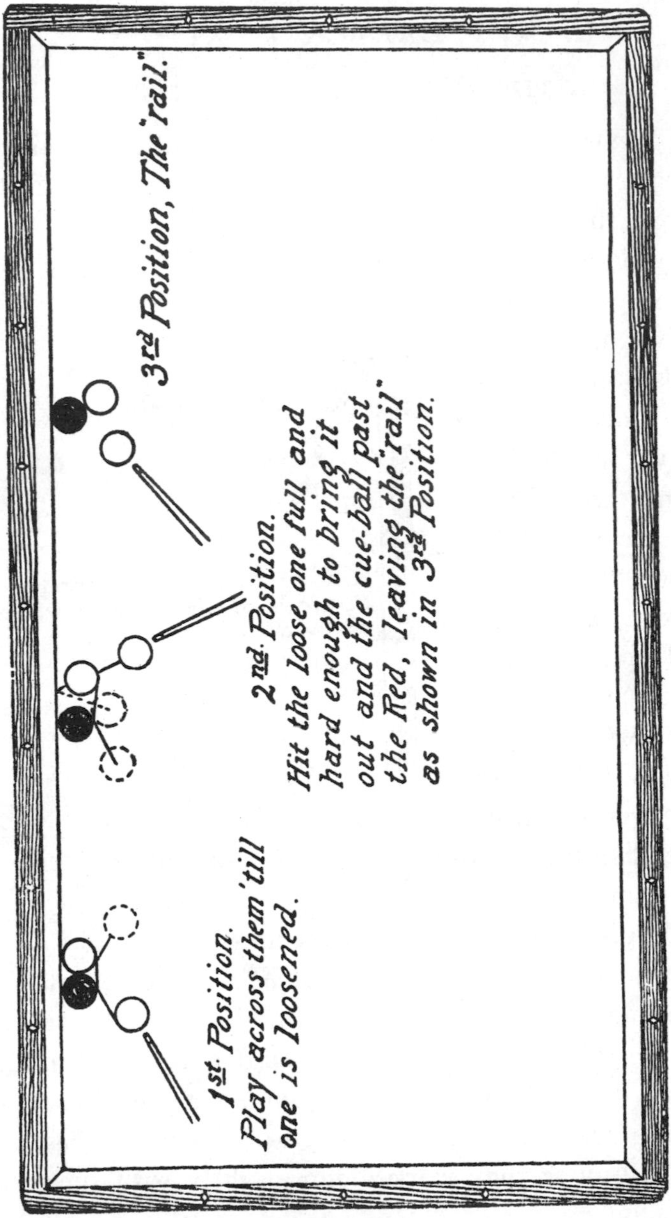

3rd Position, The "rail."

2nd. Position.
Hit the loose one full and
hard enough to bring it
out and the cue-ball past
the Red, leaving the "rail"
as shown in 3rd Position.

1st. Position.
Play across them 'till
one is loosened.

PLATE 179

Distances between positions exaggerated to show the principle. The balls remain in practically one place on the rail.

Hit Red full enough to spring it around corner. Land thin on White.

A

Soft follow. Land full on White

B

PLATE 180

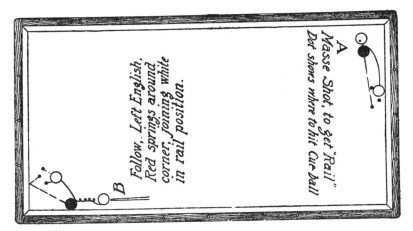

A

Masse Shot, to get "Rail"
Dot shows where to hit Cue-ball

Follow. Left English.
Red springs around
corner, joining white
in rail position.

B

PLATE 181

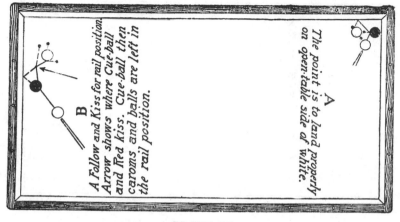

A

The point is to land properly on open-table side of white.

B

A Follow and Kiss for rail position. Arrow shows where Cue-ball and Red kiss. Cue-ball then caroms and balls are left in the rail position.

PLATE 182

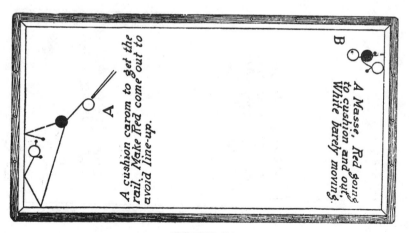

B

A Masse, Red going to cushion and out, White barely moving.

A

A cushion carom to get the rail. Make Red come out to avoid line-up.

PLATE 183

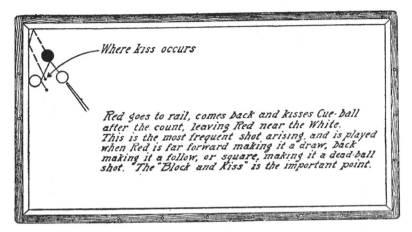

Where kiss occurs

Red goes to rail, comes back and kisses Cue-ball after the count, leaving Red near the White. This is the most frequent shot arising, and is played when Red is far forward making it a draw, back making it a follow, or square, making it a dead-ball shot. The "Block and Kiss" is the important point.

PLATE 184

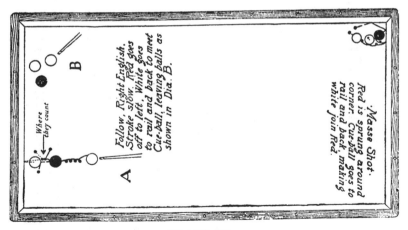

B

Where they count

Follow, Right English. Stroke slow, Red goes off to left. White goes to rail and back to meet Cue-ball, leaving balls as shown in Dia. B.

A

Masse Shot. Red is sprung around corner. Cue-ball goes to rail and back, making white join Red.

PLATE 185

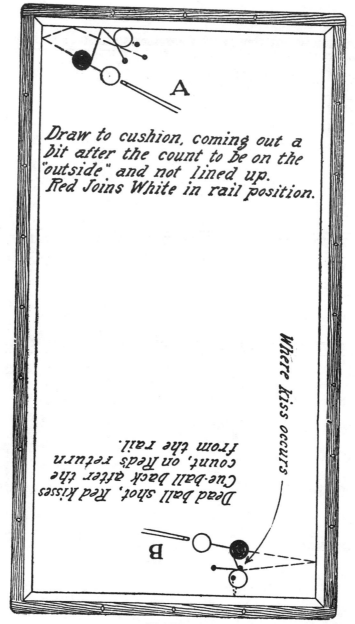

Draw to cushion, coming out a bit after the count to be on the "outside" and not lined up. Red Joins White in rail position.

Dead ball shot, Red kisses Cue-ball back after the count, on Red's return from the rail.

Where kiss occurs

PLATE 186

CHAPTER XXXII

GOOD POSITION SHOTS FROM BAD LEAVES

THERE are many positions in modern billiards that in the old days were regarded as, if not "safe" leaves, at least pretty nearly safe so far as getting a position as well as the count was concerned. Many of these today are played not only for the count, but for a resulting good position as well. Some of them are difficult to show in diagram, but a few of the more useful ones we may explain.

See Plate 187. The red ball is shown in three positions, a, b, and c. At position A you hit your cue ball "top" and left English. The left English will make the object ball "spring out" and go toward the second object ball in the corner, and the balls will gather.

In the earlier days it was customary to play this shot hard, so as to leave the balls safe if the count was not made. Now we play just hard enough to gather the balls. For nowadays safety play (except in certain cases, generally depending upon the state of the score) is regarded by fine players as poor tactics. They figure that except with uncommonly bad leaves there is better than an even chance to count. And *speed on your part*, not safety play, must be depended upon for victory. Jacob Schaefer was the first to utterly discard safety play as a standard tactic, and Ives, George Sutton, Ora Morningstar, Willie Hoppe following his footsteps

in this regard, the tactic has fallen into general dis-
repute, much to the betterment of the game.   Speed
is depended upon for winning.   A couple of good runs
and one may "put the game on ice."

In position B of the same plate (No. 187) you hit
cue ball center, or the least trifle below.   In position C
you make a draw shot of it.   In each case the first object
ball (on the rail) comes over to the corner.   Practice
will teach you the various modifications of this shot, and
the principle of springing the ball on the rail along to
a desired position comes up in a great many places,
particularly in close work along the rail and near the
corners.

Plate 188 shows two frequent shots.   The diagrams
explain them sufficiently without additional text here.

In Plate 189 we have a "Hoppe" shot.   Hitting the
red full enough, you follow to the corner, catching
the white.   The red goes across the table and to the
corner again for the gather.

In Plate 190 the follow shot is the one you are in-
clined, first off, to make.   But it loses the balls.   Drive
the red around.   Use reverse English on the cue ball to
deaden it on the cushion, landing easily on the white for
a gather.

The next series of plates (191 to 195) are of related
shots.   Similar ideas are in all of them.   The lettering
on the plates is sufficient explanation.

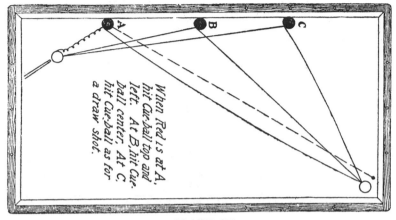

When Red is at A,
hit Cue-ball top and
left. At B, hit Cue-
ball center. At C,
hit Cue-ball as for
a draw shot.

PLATE 187

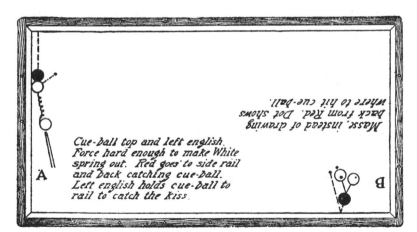

Cue-ball top and left english.
Force hard enough to make White
spring out. Red goes to side rail
and back catching cue-ball.
Left english holds cue-ball to
rail to catch the kiss.

Massé, instead of drawing
back from Red. Dot shows
where to hit cue-ball.

PLATE 188

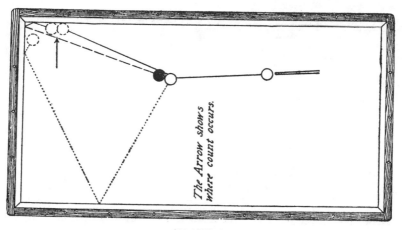

PLATE 189

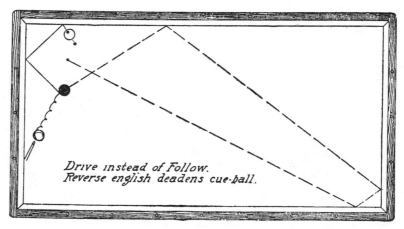

PLATE 190

The two plates (196 and 197) shown on page 226 are not like the preceding, but are well worth knowing. You, as in so many cases, knowing these, will see from them how to handle other similar ones. They show you a principle that is of

Cue-ball top, left english Hit Red full enough to get kiss, landing softly on White for draw Stroke-easy

PLATE 191

value also in leaves that do not resemble these. Some of these shots are unknown to most amateurs, and even to most of the professionals, and they will serve to get you out of many a situation that at first looks hopeless.

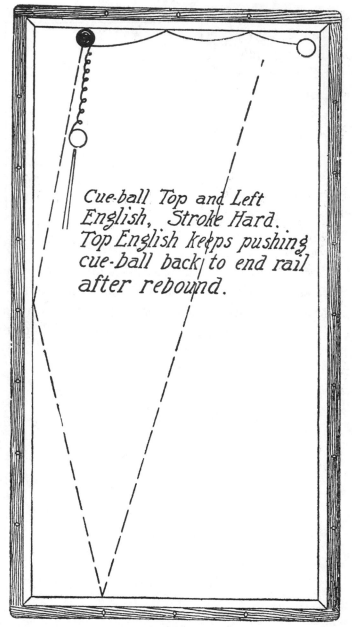

Cue-ball Top and Left English, Stroke Hard. Top English keeps pushing cue-ball back to end rail after rebound.

PLATE 192

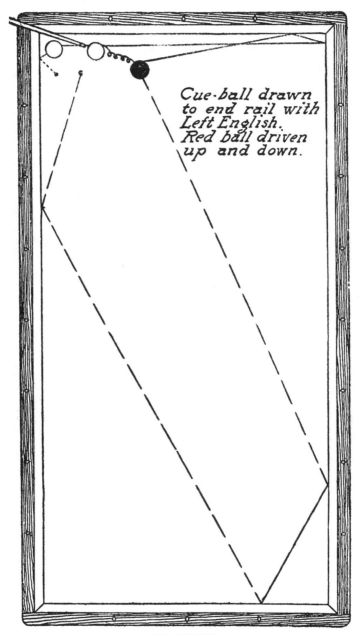

Cue-ball drawn
to end rail with
Left English.
Red ball driven
up and down.

PLATE 193

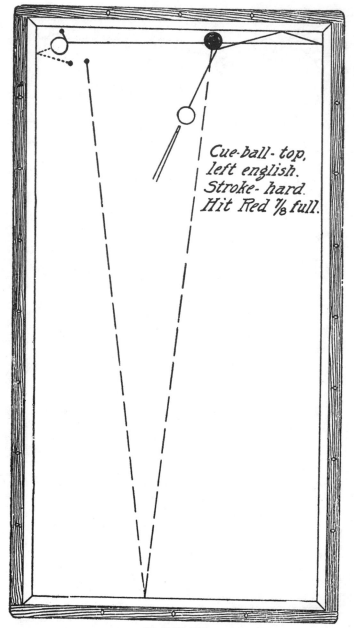

*Cue-ball-top,
left english.
Stroke-hard.
Hit Red ⅞ full.*

PLATE 194

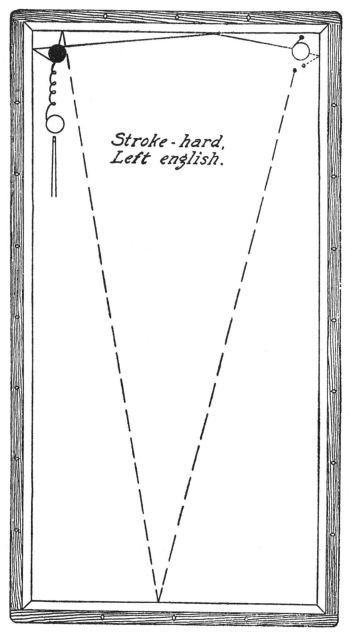

Stroke - hard,
Left english.

PLATE 195

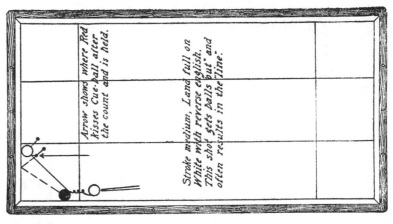

Arrow shows where Red kisses Cue-ball after the count and is held.

Stroke medium. Land full on White with reverse english. This shot gets balls "out" and often results in the "line".

PLATE 196

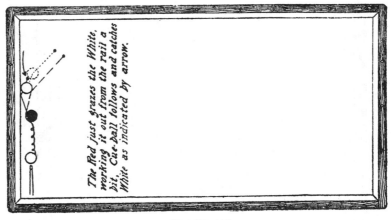

The Red just grazes the White, working it out from the rail a bit. Cue-ball follows and catches White as indicated by arrow.

PLATE 197

CHAPTER XXXIII

P LAYERS who can average, say, from four to seven
have accomplished the biggest part of billiards.
They know angles, can drive, draw, follow, massé, play
cushion and " dead-ball " shots. All that is needed for
a great increase in their speed is mastery of some minuter
technique and the attainment of greater degree of control of " speed " of shot. On the control of speed, indeed, depends — well, it is difficult to say how much does
depend upon that one thing. No position shot is good
for much if the speed be much over-done or under-done.

Greater control of speed and knowledge of the finer
points of close manipulative technique will make these 4
to 7 men good for averages of 15 or better. But it is just
here that they fail. They do not know how to " manipulate." I do not mean that they cannot stroke softly.

What " Manipulation " Is.— Manipulation is the art
of making both balls move exactly to certain desirable
places, and necessary to it, as a precedent, is the knowledge of what the desirable points are. *Delicacy alone
is not manipulation.*

A study of the finer technique is the most interesting
part of billiards, and, once grasped, will make any " five-
man " a possible " fifteen-man."

On " Going Through."— It is so often desirable, when the balls are close together, but *facing the open table,* or *too far from the end rails,* to "go through," and so needful is it that in so doing the balls be not "lost," that practice on this one thing is extremely desirable.

Place the balls, for instance, as shown in Plate 198, frozen or very close together. They are too far up the table and you wish to go through them and come back.

The danger point is on the *very first shot* of this going-through process. The balls must be hit so softly that, while not leaving the cue ball frozen to either object ball, the object balls, nevertheless, after the first shot, are not to exceed about $2\frac{3}{8}$ inches (the diameter of a ball) apart. Have that distance in mind as the extent of separation that will exist *when the actual " going-through " shot is made,* and work the separation slowly up to that distance.

Generally this is best attained by hitting *one object ball fuller than the other* in making the soft shots and landing "dead" on the second ball, and *stopping very near it.* Then nearly all the motion is imparted to one *ball,* and is more easily calculated and controlled.

When the actual shot to go through is made the cue ball just *barely grazes* and *hardly moves* at least one of the object balls, and perhaps both are just grazed, and they are left still very close together.

Be Sure to Get Past.— But, in going through, the cue ball must go far enough *to get past the center of the object ball,* that is, " above it," so that both object balls are toward the end rail or corners nearest you. Don't leave the cue ball in the middle (the dotted outline shown in

Diagram B of Plate 198) or you will be forced to make a massé shot or go to the cushion, with the greatest danger of loss of control.

Sometimes it is desirable to get *past* the balls, so as to have cue ball out in the open-table side of them and then work them back toward the end or a corner. You may be too far away to " go through " first making a very soft carom, but you can " go past."

Plate 199 shows how to do it. This position has variations in table position, in d i s t a n c e apart, etc., etc. But the possibility of this kind of a shot often arises. It is also often used to avoid lining the balls up, as shown elsewhere.

Here, too, is another point that the first-class player bears in mind in close work, and particularly in working along the line.

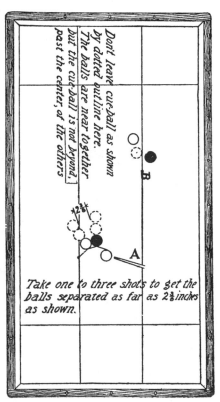

PLATE 198

The distance that the balls travel is exaggerated to make the principle plain. They actually move only the minutest fraction of an inch.

English on the cue ball affects the object ball, *not only on the cushion*, but also on its *course to the cushion*.

For instance, place the balls as shown in Plate 200. A shows (in exaggerated form, to make the point clear) the effect of English on the object ball. Some say it is the cue ball that swerves. I won't quarrel about that. The point is that *you may, by shifting English, force the object ball to sidle about at will*, with the result that you get it just where you want it for the next shot.

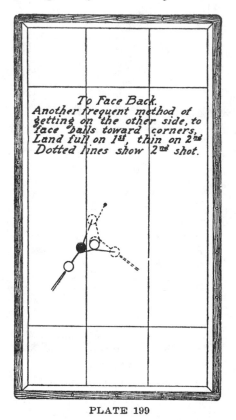

To Face Back.
Another frequent method of getting on the other side, to face balls toward corners. Land full on 1st, thin on 2nd Dotted lines show 2nd shot.

PLATE 199

In B is shown a position when working on the line. This diagram and diagram C show the opposite effect of opposite English, one leaving the balls perfect for the drive, the other losing the position for the drive to the cushion.

This serves to make the point. The application comes in numerous forms whenever you have close-nursing manipulation on hand.

Now, right here, having shown how the English swerves the object ball in soft shots, is the place to point out where most amateurs, and, indeed, some professionals, fail in getting the best results out of the balk-line nurse.

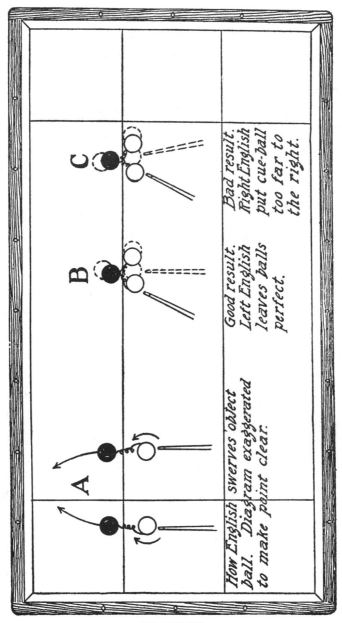

A

How English swerves object ball. Diagram exaggerated to make point clear.

B

Good result. Left English leaves balls perfect.

C

Bad result. Right English put cue-ball too far to the right.

PLATE 200

In playing this nurse you must put a high value ON EVERY INCH of distance. Avoid sending the first object ball *too far from the line* when preparing to drive it to the cushion and back.

If the object ball, of this drive, is over two inches from the cue ball, it is a distinct *draw* shot. If it is inside the two-inch distance, it is almost a dead-ball shot, or a *very slight* draw. Some call it a "concussion shot;" that is, the natural elasticity of the ivory on concussion alone is all that is needed to make the cue ball come back for a very short distance. And you do not have to hit the cue ball low enough to *risk a miscue*.

Again, as you do not have to make the cue ball travel far, you can the more easily make it land perfectly.

First Step.— So, then, bear in mind the effect of English in swerving the first object ball to the proper place so that the drive and draw is straight instead of at an angle. For that "drive and draw" shot, in its control, is the keystone shot of the line-nurse. On its perfection depends the continuation of the perfect line position. There is not much danger of the player missing the soft carom shots, but there is great danger of his making the drive and draw badly.

Second Step.— In making your shots preparatory to getting the drive-and-draw position bear in mind where you want the three balls to stand *when making the draw*.

See Plate 201. Diagram 1 shows a series of positions you *do not want*. The lettering in each diagram tells what is bad about the position. At the end is the *position you do want* when making the "drive-and-draw." Note well the right-angled-triangle situation.

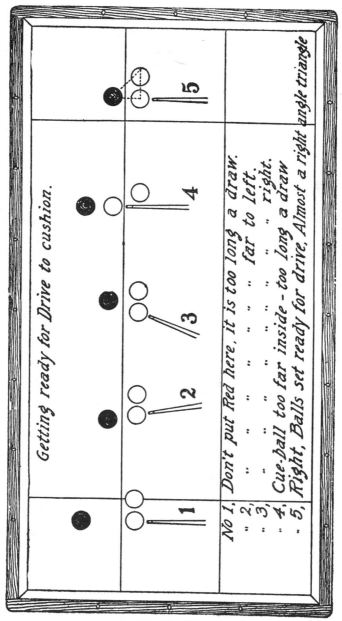

Getting ready for Drive to cushion.

No 1, Don't put Red here, it is too long a draw.
" 2, " " " " far to left.
" 3, " " " " right.
" 4, Cue-ball too far inside - too long a draw
" 5, Right, Balls set ready for drive, Almost a right angle triangle

PLATE 201

See, also, Plate 202 for positions *you do not want to result from the " drive-and-draw "* and how they happened. The last one of the series shows the *position you do want* to result from the " drive-and-draw."

Third Step.—Now, nothing is more important in making the " drive-and-draw " than this:

DO NOT DEPEND TOO MUCH UPON THE CUE BALL BLOCKING THE RETURNING OB-

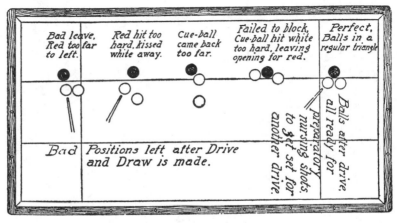

PLATE 202

JECT BALL PERFECTLY. Therefore, do not hit the object ball on the " drive-and-draw " shot any harder than ENOUGH TO JUST GET IT BACK to place. A very slight kiss will do no damage. A kiss perfectly in the middle of the cue ball will not hurt. BUT THAT IS TOO SMALL A MARK to depend on hitting it perfectly, and having the driven object come back swiftly enough to wreck things, if the exact center be not hit, is bad.

If it comes back slowly, just barely getting to the line,

it may have a side-to-side variation of from $2\frac{1}{2}$ to even 3 inches and still leave you in control for a continuation of the line-nurse.

To George Sutton must be given credit for perfecting this method of playing the line-nurse. In the old days we used to trust, almost entirely, to the kiss to stop the returning object ball. Now we play also to get the speed just right.

On "Blocking."— As a rule, on drives to the cushion, try whenever possible to "block." That is, leave the cue ball and second object ball right together, so that when the first object ball returns it HAS THE WIDTH OF TWO BALLS IN ITS PATH, instead of one; that is, nearly 5 inches of ivory instead of $2\frac{1}{2}$. It is, in fact, more than that; it is $7\frac{1}{8}$ inches, for the returning ball has to be considered, too.

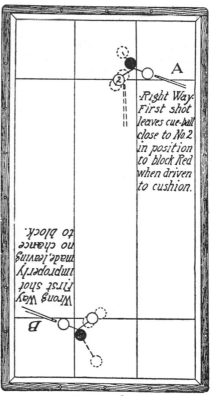

A

Right Way.
First shot
leaves cue-ball
close to No 2
in position
to block Red
when driven
to cushion.

Wrong Way.
First shot
improperly
made, leaving
no chance
to block.

B

PLATE 203

To work this properly, sometimes the first shot must be so made that the "block" is possible on the second shot.

Plate 203 shows an example. In A the first shot is properly made. In B no "blocking" possibility is left, because the first shot was improperly made, the cue ball knocking the second object ball too far away.

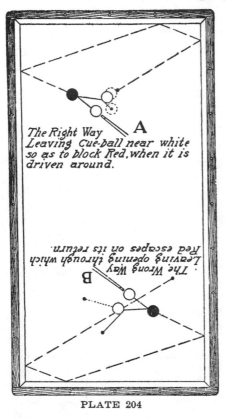

The Right Way **A**
Leaving Cue-ball near white so as to block Red, when it is driven around.

The Wrong Way
Leaving opening through which Red escapes on its return.
B

PLATE 204

Plate 204 shows a longer drive, with the same point of "blocking" brought out.

More on Close Manipulation.— Plate 205 shows a position in which the required shot will be found valuable not only here, but in many other places on the table. The point is to make a soft shot, letting the cue ball count, but stay back of carom ball, so as to leave "the thin shot" for the next. For in making the thin shot in close billiards one may manipulate the balls in many ways and land on the object ball where he will.

Now, here is an important point about this leave. (Plate 205.) Sometimes the original position is such that the first shot may be made on either ball. If you wish the ultimate line position resulting from this preliminary

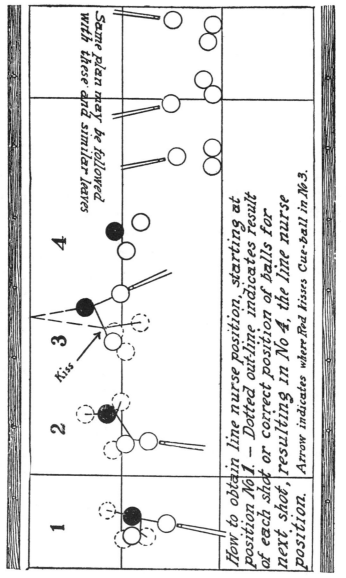

PLATE 205

Position No. 2 shows the balls as they lay after No. 1; No. 3 shows position after No. 2, etc., etc. The balls move very little, distances being exaggerated in the drawing.

manipulation, to face the corner on your left play on the *right* object ball first, and *vice versa*. [Note.— In Plate 205, position No. 2 shows balls in position resulting from shot at position No. 1, and so on.]

Stay Near the Ends of the Table.— This shot is one that is valuable not only near the line, but anywhere on the table, for it will enable you to "turn" the balls toward a corner when you find yourself headed for the " open sea " of mid-table.

A variation of this shot that is useful sometimes occurs when the balls lie as shown in Plate 206, the need being to get the balls out of balk. Drive ball No. 1 out, landing so softly on No. 2 as to leave "the thin shot." On the next land on ball No. 1 so as to leave a draw for position.

Concerning the " Thin Shot."— I have spoken often about the "thin shot," meaning, of course, with the balls close together, a chance to touch the edge of the first ball, landing on the second ball *just where you want to*. And that is the reason of its value. (See Plate 207.) You may want to land for a draw; you may want to land for another thin shot (the "edge-nurse") or for a " going-through" shot. You may do as you will. The long, thin shot is not desirable, and a very long one is bad.

In all close work, especially near the cushions, the thin shot is valuable and always to be kept in mind, to work the balls so that it may be left up.

Another point: in some cases you have the choice of landing full on the second ball and then draw, or to land to leave the thin shot, make it, and then draw. Don't

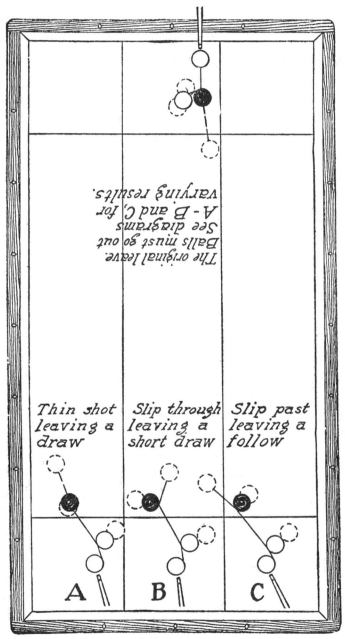

The original leave.
Balls must go out
See diagrams
A - B and C, for
varying results.

Thin shot leaving a draw

Slip through leaving a short draw

Slip past leaving a follow

A   B   C

PLATE 206

you see that *that is just one extra count* from the given leave? The sum of these *extra counts* in a close match may be the difference between victory and defeat. It is always a percentage in your favor.

In " going through," if you take four or five in doing it and the other fellow gets through in three shots, you have two shots the best of it, a goodly percentage in your favor, for the going through-shot is likely to happen many times in the course of a game. In big championships, 500 points, it might well come up ten or fifteen times. Two or three extra points each time are not to be sneezed at.

This was one of Frank Ives' percentages over most other players. I have seen him take seven or eight shots to get through, and even Schaefer rarely took over five. And this point of getting *extra points* before driving ("don't drive until you have to") applies not only to the "going-through" shot, but to soft shots along the rail, with balls astride the line, the player preparing to drive one to the cushion and back. And again to the line position itself. Each time you manipulate the balls preparing for the "drive-and-draw" there's a chance to pick up an extra point or two by careful work.

Plate 207 shows a position where landing thin not only gives you the extra point, but gives you a better chance of saving control in making the second shot, for you may land on the second ball full or thin, as you choose.

Elevated Cue Butt.— In connection with this point of close manipulation, where it is desired that the object balls be moved very slightly, I may call attention to a

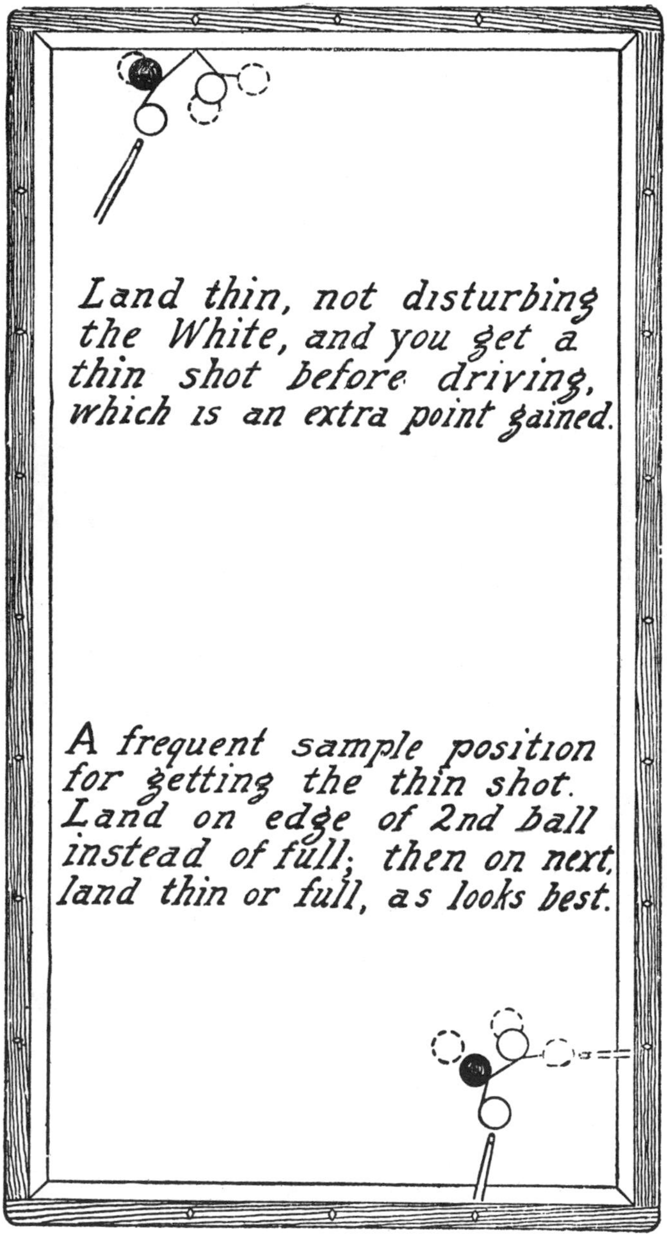

Land thin, not disturbing the White, and you get a thin shot before driving, which is an extra point gained.

A frequent sample position for getting the thin shot. Land on edge of 2nd ball instead of full; then on next, land thin or full, as looks best.

PLATE 207

matter of technique that is helpful and therefore important.

Take the "edge"-nurse, for instance; the object balls side by side, the cue ball passing across their face. In making this stroke elevate the butt of your cue a bit, so that the shot has a touch of "drag." The cue ball starts with speed enough to prevent its rolling off. Then the "drag" takes effect and the ball slows up quickly.

No ivory ball was ever exactly perfect for more than a very brief time, even minutes serving to expand or con-

PLATE 208

Elevating butt of cue to get drag on the cue ball in soft close shots

tract it in varying temperatures. And in this close work the deflection of the sixty-fourth part of an inch in the course of the ball makes the difference between a perfect shot and a poor one.

Another thing that will help in this soft "edging" is a firmer grip on the butt of the cue. The cue ball gets more action from a loose grip and less from a tight grip.

Plate 208 shows cue position in making these soft shots. The French players have developed this point more of late than the Americans, and have made it of great value in nursing.   But it takes practice, for the "feel" is different.

The same elevation of cue butt is also useful in short and medium draw shots.   It is perfect for the little "nip" draw used in the line-nurse.   In this the French players also favor the tighter grip, as giving a deader ball and better control of force than the loose grip.   It is with this little "nip" stroke that George Sutton at his best (as, for instance, when he beat Willie Hoppe and averaged an even 100) showed his mastery of the line-nurse.   The shot, when delivered, feels something like a "near-massé."   You can get quick draw action while hitting the cue ball high enough so that miscues need not worry you.   Willie Hoppe's "dig," as George Slosson terms it, is a perfect example of this style of stroke.

CHAPTER XXXIV

USEFUL POINTS ON CERTAIN FREQUENT LEAVES

CLOSELY related to what I have just said on close manipulation come some points bearing on the best method of making certain shots that frequently arise, yet have unusual features. The point is not only to get the count, but to get it in the best way either to avoid a tie-up or to slip in one additional point over the usual and more obvious method of play.

Sometimes the thing is to "block" the object ball on its return from the cushion after a drive. This almost always is attained by landing dead on the second ball. Sometimes the point is landing on the best spot.

Notice the leave in Diagram B in Plate 209. In making the shot try to have the count *completed before* the first ball *gets back* from the cushion, so that when it kisses the cue ball the latter will not be knocked against the second ball and spoil the leave. Also, try to land on the second ball *on the edge nearest you.*

In Diagram A, Plate 209, you try to land as thin as possible on the edge nearest you, playing almost as though you were trying to get too much draw and miss the shot.

When both balls are so placed as to be under control, but near the center of the end rail (that is, far from the

A

Complete the count before Red gets back, so that the kiss will not knock Cue-ball against the White and spoil the leave.

Land on white as thin as possible. Plenty of draw and right twist.

B

PLATE 209

line), it is often best to get them near the line *on the very first shot*. See Plate 210.

On the second shot you can land softly and retain

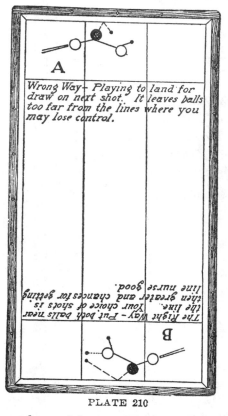

A

Wrong Way— Playing to land for draw on next shot. It leaves balls too far from the lines where you may lose control.

B

The Right Way — Put both balls near the line. Your choice of shots is then greater and chances for getting line nurse good.

PLATE 210

control. If you wait till the second shot to put them over the line (having made the first shot softly), you are likely to hit them too hard in order to be sure to get over, and have an awkward, bad-angled shot for the next.

When they are both in the middle section at the end of the table work them toward the line *that is nearest*.

Whenever the balls are close to the corner, in 18.2 balk-line, *be sure to get one near the line on the first shot*. Plate 211 shows four such positions. They arise in great variety. Bad tie-ups will often result from failure to get the balls near the line *on the first shot*, waiting, instead, until the second, yet beginners at balk-line almost invariably overlook the point. I know of no more frequent error, and I have observed players in amateur championships do this with disastrous results.

Positions where the point is to get near the line on the first shot.

PLATE 211

On all follow shots down the table try to avoid line-ups. Two such shots are shown in Plate 212.

Two Follow Shots
To avoid a "line-up," be sure
to get Red back far enough.

PLATE 212

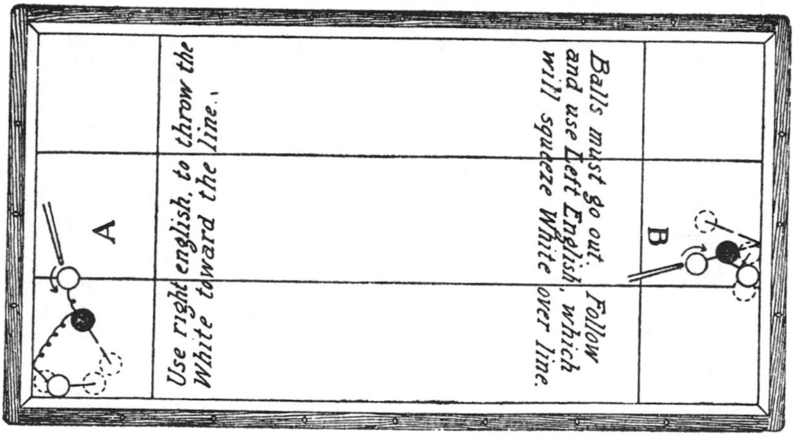

Use right english, to throw the
White toward the line.

A

Balls must go out. Follow
and use Left English, which
will squeeze White over line.

B

PLATE 213

The effect of English on the second ball, if borne in mind, can be made useful often in getting the second ball "out" or "loosened" from the cushion without endangering control, which a bank shot is so likely to do.

Plate 213 shows two examples of this.

Frequently the kiss, either before or after the count, can be made to hold the balls in place, this being better than to risk a bank shot.   Plate 214 shows two examples.

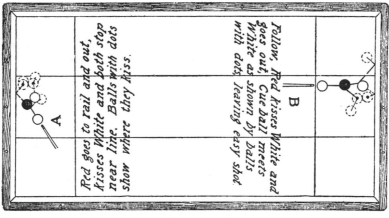

PLATE 214

Plate 215 shows a close draw where a "nip" draw, if landed (not too thin) on the side of the second object ball nearest you, will be more likely to give the thin shot or easy cushion carom, instead of a drive or draw at a bad angle, or a shot that will face the balls up the table.

In making short, easy cushion shots it is often of the greatest importance to land near the edge, instead of full, to avoid a tie-up.   Plate 216 shows a common example.

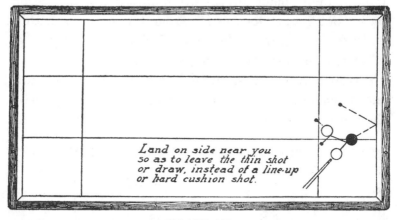

*Land on side near you
so as to leave the thin shot
or draw, instead of a line-up
or hard cushion shot.*

PLATE 215

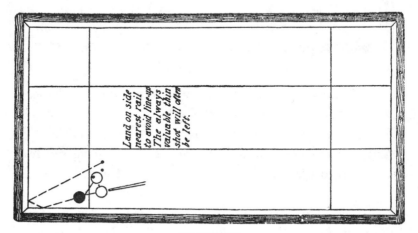

*Land on side
nearest rail
to avoid line-up.
The always
valuable thin
shot will often
be left.*

PLATE 216

Plate 217 shows the balls in a position where the ordinary draw is likely to line up the balls. Draw to the

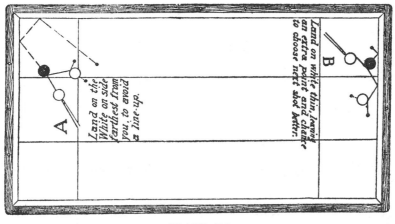

Land on the White on side farthest from you, to avoid a line-up.

Land on white thin, leaving an extra point and chance to choose next shot better.

A

B

PLATE 217

side of the second ball nearest the side rail. This shot, properly made, is likely to leave an easy drive and draw for the line position.

CHAPTER XXXV

ON THE VALUE OF THE INCH

THE one thing that most distinctly marks the difference between the fair player and the fine player is in the matter of valuation of the inches. I am constantly telling young players, "*Don't give away the*

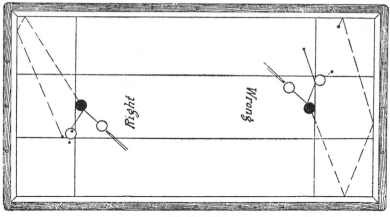

PLATE 218

A good shot to practice to acquire control of speed.

inches!" Often they give away, needlessly, not only inches, but feet.

The value of the "dead" ball is in saving the inches, and the dead-ball stroke in varying forms, both direct ball-to-ball and off the cushion, is the most distinguishing feature of the expert's mastery. It is one of the finest shots in the game.

In the notes on "Primary Position Play" I drew

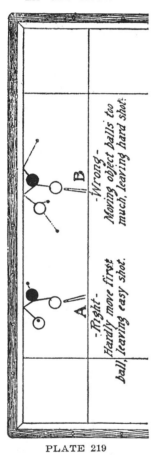

attention to the necessity of the soft shot when the two object balls are very close together, the cue ball moving them, on contact, only a fraction of an inch, instead of two or three inches. The same point arises in countless forms, and a few in diagram will serve to impress it and make it clearer. The first one is in the form of an ordinary gathering shot, in Plate 218.

The good player, in all such cases, takes the greatest pains not only to make the shot, but to get the balls "under his hand," as we say. (See Plate 218.) The careless player aims to make the count and get the balls "somewhere around." This is one of the grosser forms of "giving away the inches." It arises in all

PLATE 219   drives for a gather. The finer forms come in close manipulation. In the balk-line nurse the value of the inch is of the greatest importance, the difference of a quarter of an inch often making the difference between a good shot and a bad shot.

In Chapter Sixteen, on "Close Manipulation," I have

called attention to the value of the inch in the little shots preparatory to the "drive-and-draw" on the line. If the cue ball is within an inch or two of the object ball it is the easiest kind of a draw, with no chance for a miscue, and an easy chance to land perfectly and dead. If, however, the cue ball is three inches from the driven object ball, the draw is long enough to endanger getting the

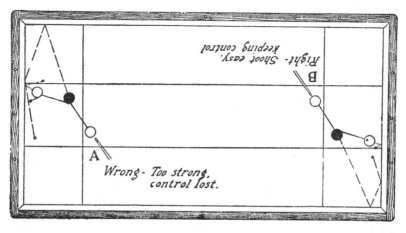

PLATE 220

exact amount of force, and, if too great, breaking up the nurse; or, in the effort not to get too great speed, of digging too deeply on the cue ball and making a miscue.

Plate 219 shows another common shot. The point is to hit the first ball so thin that you just "graze the glisten" and let the English carry the cue ball along to the carom ball, leaving an easy draw.

The succeeding plates (220 to 222) are self-explanatory.

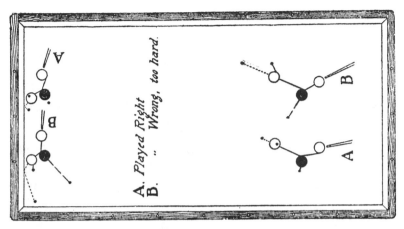

PLATE 221

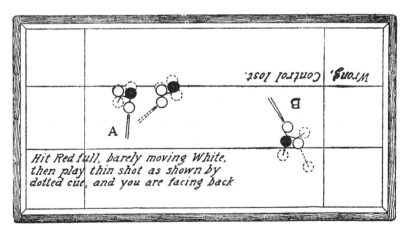

PLATE 222

CHAPTER XXXVI

COMPARATIVE THEORY OF STRAIGHT RAIL, BALK-LINE AND CUSHION CAROMS

I N STRAIGHT-RAIL billiards there is just one great nursing position to work for — the rail-nurse. You plan every shot with the idea of getting the balls ultimately to the corners or the end rail, close together. Anywhere along or inside of the five-inch line shown in our study diagrams of the line-nurse, and especially at the ends of the table, where the expert is almost certain to get the balls on the rail in a few shots.

Plate 223 is a straight-rail map. *The depth of the shading is greatest in those portions of the table where it is most advantageous to get the balls.* Near the corners the shading is heaviest, as there the nearness of both rails gives more manipulative chances, not only to get the balls on the rail, but also to *regain control* if they begin to get balky, as billiard balls have a way of doing. The map as shown should not be so dark along the middle of the side rails. That place is good only when the balls are in line-nurse position, or under control in some other way.

It is only at the ends of the table that one has a good chance to stop balky balls from their antics. In mid-table the balls have all the best of it.

Down the side rail is good in the rail-nurse so long as

256

PLATE 223

STRAIGHT RAIL MAP

Depth of shading shows desirability of location for nursing purposes. Best gathering points are near the corners. "Rail nurse" can be played all around the table when once the position is gained.

the balls are acting well.   But if, to correct an error, you
have to drive to the cushion and back, your drive is long.
At the end rails it is short.

Now, in balk-line, as will be noted in the balk-line
maps, further on, the choice positions are *not* close in
the *corners.*   They are, in fact, danger spots.   Along
the end balk-lines or along the end rails *near the side
balk-lines* are the best positions.   Hence, with a given

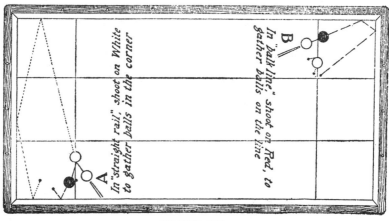

PLATE 224

leave, such as is shown in Plate 224, the best shot in
*straight rail is one thing and in balk-line billiards is
another.*   One might draw scores of diagrams to illustrate this point.   But a careful study of the difference
between the choice places on the straight-rail map and
on the balk-line maps will direct you in your choice of
shots.   Keep the balls *headed toward the parts of the
table shown in heaviest shade* on the straight rail map.
(Plate 223.)

In balk-line, except for the possibilities, always to be

kept in mind, of getting the "chuck" or "anchor" (the latter is now barred in championships), it is the best of tactics to *keep going for the line.* Keep the balls as *near the lines* as you can, so that when you have to cross them you do not have far to go and can *save the inches.*

There are only two really good contact points for the " chuck "-nurse, where the reach is easy, and there are a great many places where the line-nurse is to be attained.

Yet not all line positions are equally desirable. In general, the best positions, that is, the positions where, *in case of the balls getting balky, you have more ways to turn,* more opportunities for getting them under perfect control again, are:

First — The end rails, near the points where the two long balk-lines touch the end rails. I call these the "contact points."

Second — The portions of the balk-lines from the cushion-contact point out to the intersection with the other lines.

High Value of the End Rails. — I regard the point of keeping at the end rails as of the *very highest* importance. This territory is worth 50 per cent more than any other, and fully 100 per cent better than that part of the table between the spots. Around the end rails you have many lines of retreat and attack, many ways to prevent the run being stopped. *No great runs were ever made anywhere else.* BAD POSITIONS IN MID-TABLE ARE OFTEN GOOD POSITIONS AT THE END RAILS.

PLATE 225

BALK LINE MAP (18.2)

Darkest shaded places have the highest strategic value in position play. Note the value marks (approximate) = 100, 75, and 50.

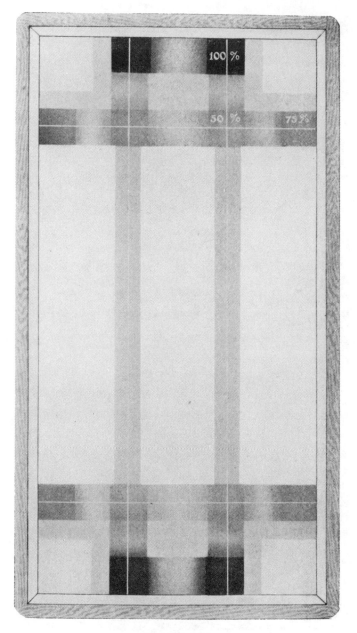

PLATE 226

BALK LINE MAP (18.1)

Darkest shaded places have the highest strategic value
in position play. Corners and side spaces are even more
dangerous in 18.1 than in 18.2. Note the value marks (approximate)=100, 75, and 50.

To win billiard matches you must keep the other fellow sitting in his chair.

Difference Between 18.2 and 18.1.— See Plates 225 and 226, which are balk-line maps, worked out by the editor of this volume, something, so far as my billiard experience goes, entirely new as a means of putting position billiards strikingly before the eye. The first one is an 18.2 map. The next is an 18.1 map. In 18.1 the corners are much more to be avoided than in 18.2, for in 18.2 you have the great advantage of a preparatory shot. The same thing applies to the long spaces down the side rails. There, in 18.1, you are in the very greatest danger of losing control, for you must get out of balk on the very first shot; so in 18.1 THE SIDE PANELS are VERY BAD.

In fact, in 18.1 the side spaces are much worse than the mid-table space, for in the side spaces you must drive at once, and, if the balls are facing up-table, it is generally a nasty drive, with little or no position possibility in it.

In 18.2 the side spaces are a *little better* than the mid-table space, for you have the preparatory shot; next, you are nearer the cushion for cross-table work; and, lastly, the up-and-down table drives are likely to be helped by having the side rail near by to help guide the driven object ball back to a better place.

In 18.1, too, the importance of keeping *as near as possible to the balk-lines* in all portions of the table is much greater, so as to have short shots to get across. But in all forms of balk-line one cannot repeat too often that *the end rail positions, and especially around the contact points and near the balk-lines, are, from all points of view, the best.*

The end-rail contact points are fully 25 per cent more valuable than the side-rail contact points.

To give the idea clearly I should rate the comparative strategic values (approximately) of the three best table-localities, as follows, in balk-line:

1 — End-rail "contact points".... 100 (best possible)
2 — Side-rail "contact points"... 75 (second best)
3 — Where lines intersect........ 50 (third choice)

But in the 18.1 game the balk-line intersection points are favored by some players at a higher value.

In the 18.1 map it will be noticed that the dangerous territory of the side-rail spaces comes up to the cross-table lines, and the corner spaces are bad to a distance farther from the exact corner than in 18.2, for, having to cross the line on the first shot, the distance may be enough to lose control, even though it be only eight or ten inches, while in 18.2 there is the preparatory in which to get one ball near a line.

As good as the side-rail contact points are, there is "the open sea" of the mid-table on one side of them. On the end rails, when the need comes — *and it always will come!* — to drive or bank, it is the shortest drive or bank on the table, instead of the longest. On the end rail you *may work either side of the balls,* slipping through, if you wish, driving to either cushion, and in general have much the best of it.

Avoid the long drive. You cannot tell about its last six inches.

Avoid the Mid-Table.— I am firmly of the belief that when you get the balls as far from the end rails as, say, between the cross-table balk-lines and the spot it is time to get them headed back on the first sign of their breaking away from control. Do it either by going through or by playing for a draw position, or by any other means that look good; *but do it!*

Do your best to keep away from the middle of the table, more even in 18.2 than in 18.1. There, when you have to make any shot, you have to make it perfectly, or have a dangerous leave, and no man living can keep on making perfect shots all the time. And when you have to make a mid-table recovery shot you have 50 per cent the worst of it at the start, *no matter how well you can execute.*

How to Get Away from Mid-Table.— Generally, when in mid-table, the balls can best be sent to the end of the table by making first a preparatory shot for a succeeding draw up and down the table, driving the object ball up and back, and *landing on the carom ball " above."* Be sure to get the driven ball back beyond the other or the shot fails its purpose.

Of course, if the balls are in fine position for easy control and some cheap points, such as can be made on the " edge-nurse," of the line-nurse, or something as good, *get the easy ones first. But in mid-table be on the lookout for signs of losing control.*

When loss of control in mid-table threatens, give the balls the benefit of the doubt and play to get back toward the end *as soon as possible.*

Only recently I observed a man who has held professional championships stick to play in mid-table when the balls worked badly instead of working them back to the end, with the result that twice within a short time, the balls getting unruly, he was left to make a cushion shot or bank shot. He made the shots, *but he lost control,* and his runs were broken. *In both of these instances the leaves he got would have been comparatively easy had they occurred at the ends instead of in the center of the table.*

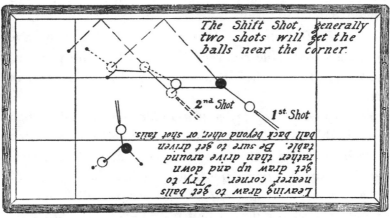

The Shift Shot, generally two shots will get the balls near the corner.

2ⁿᵈ Shot   1ˢᵗ Shot

ball back beyond other, or shot fails. table. Be sure to get driven rather than drive around get draw up and down nearer corner. Try to Leaving draw to get balls

PLATE 227

There are many ways of getting back to the end, depending upon the position of the balls, and the more obvious will readily occur to you.

In Plate 227 we show the "shift shot," a series of plain caroms, not often more than two, by which the balls can be worked from mid-table toward the end rapidly.

In Plates 228 and 229 we show leaves which in mid-table are dangerous. The SAME LEAVES, NEAR

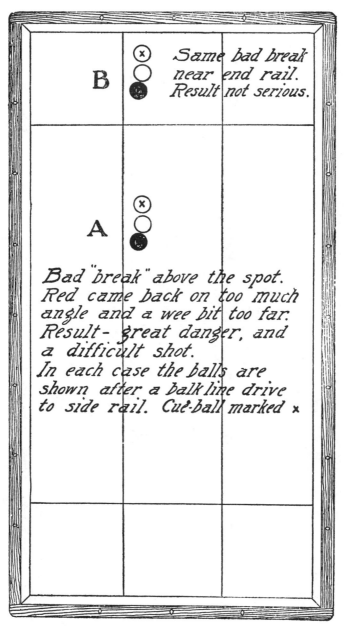

B   *Same bad break near end rail. Result not serious.*

A

Bad "break" above the spot. Red came back on too much angle and a wee bit too far. Result - great danger, and a difficult shot. In each case the balls are shown after a balk line drive to side rail. Cue-ball marked x

PLATE 228

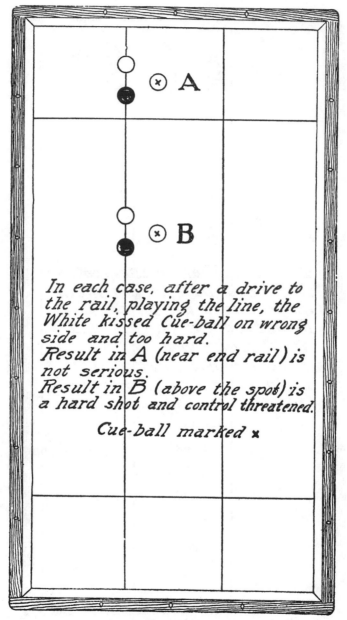

In each case, after a drive to
the rail, playing the line, the
White kissed Cue-ball on wrong
side and too hard.
Result in A (near end rail) is
not serious.
Result in B (above the spot) is
a hard shot and control threatened.

Cue-ball marked **x**

PLATE 229

THE END RAILS, ARE NOT DANGEROUS. One could make a great many such diagrams.

Take my advice, Mr. Youthful Billiard Player, keep to the ends of the table. When away from there *get back* as soon as you can without throwing away the very easy ones, where the balls are "under the hand."

The Choice of Contact Points.— Many cases will arise where you have the choice of gathering the balls at the "contact points" (where the balk-lines touch the rails), either on the side rail or on the end rail, as you may prefer. ALWAYS CHOOSE THE END RAIL CONTACT POINTS. Always, however, keep the cue ball *with* the object balls in getting to the contact points, thus avoiding drives or dangers of "roll-off" or line-up. Leaving the cue ball even a foot away from the object balls is likely to be a serious matter.

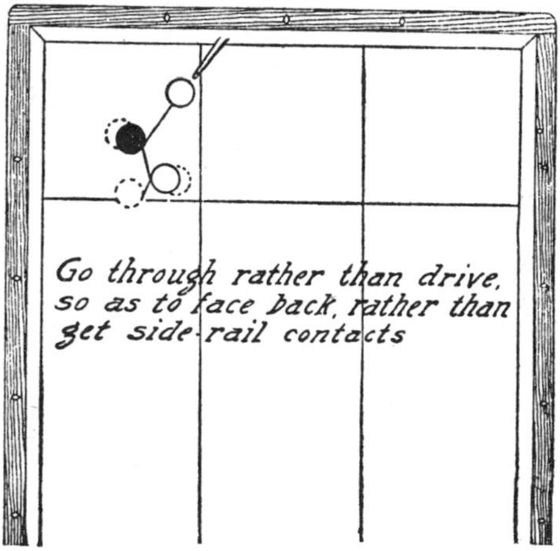

Go through rather than drive, so as to face back, rather than get side-rail contacts

PLATE 230

Any opportunity that offers to get to the end rail, either by slipping through, or by easy massé, or by easy bank is worth while.

Plate 230 shows a position where one shot (draw from the red) will prepare for gathering near the side rail line, the other for heading back to the end rail.

The other shot — the one indicated in the plate — is the "slip through," which will leave the balls headed toward the end rail contact points. *Take that one!*

Plate 231 shows a position where you must choose between the end rail contact points. Here the draw is too long to hold the balls to the *near* contact point, so you draw and prepare to take them to the *far* contact point (b).

Take the line of least resistance. That is, choose the shot you can make most surely. Pick the shot you can make with a *good solid blow*, instead of the one that requires too much draw, with chance of miscues, or indeed any shot that verges on the wonderful in execution. Let the other fellow do the marvelous ones. Take the eight-inch draw in preference to the two-foot draw always *if the chances of good leave are anywhere near equal.* The count is first in importance, the exactness of position second.

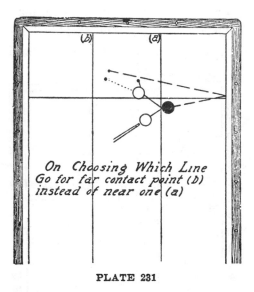

On Choosing Which Line
Go for far contact point (b)
instead of near one (a)

PLATE 231

Bad Positions in 18.1. — I have spoken about the difference in corner position in 18.1 and 18.2, they being the more dangerous in 18.1. For that reason, at the

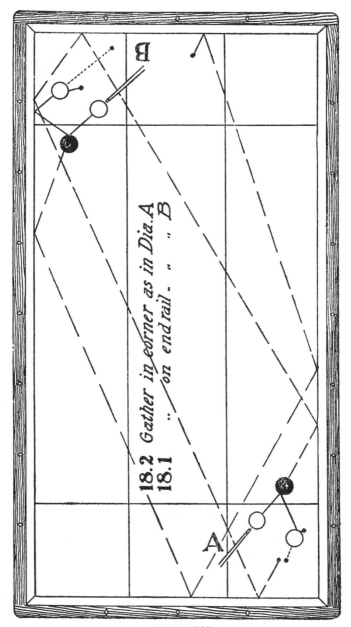

18.2 Gather in corner as in Dia. A
18.1 " " on end rail. " " B

PLATE 232

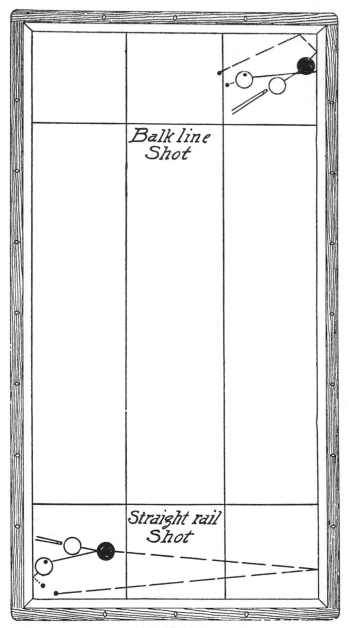

PLATE 233

beginning of your inning if you have an open table gathering shot and one way of making it will gather the balls in the corner, the other at the end rails nearer the middle, take the latter in 18.1. In 18.2 you should try for the corner gather on long drives, having better chances both to get the gather and handle the balls if too close in. Plate 232 shows an example.

In this plate in A (18.2) you play a dead ball drive and gather near the corner. In B (18.1) you go to the cushion and gather the balls near the end rail.

Briefly, here are your tactics:

In straight rail go for the corners.

In 18.2 go for the end rail contact points and on long gather shots take a chance for the corners.

In 18.1 keep away from the corners and side rail squares. Go for the balk-lines and the end rail squares near the contact points.

Plate 233 gives another simple instance of varying choice shots in rail and balk-line play from the same position.

Position Play in Cushion Caroms.— In cushion caroms the general line of strategy is the reverse, one may say, of the strategy in balk-line. Instead of carrying both balls along and keeping them "ahead" of you, it is often best to leave one ball behind, so as to get a cushion carom leave. You generally plan to leave one ball at least near a cushion, and preferably near a corner. But, as in straight rail, you keep playing toward corners.

In cushion caroms the "rub-nurse" is the grand position, having the standing of the "rail-nurse" in straight billiards, of the "line-nurse" in balk-line billiards.

CHAPTER XXXVII

DON'TS, DO'S, AND POINTS ON PRACTICE

SOME hints from a life-time of billiard experience may not come amiss as to preparation for competition billiards.

In your practice work especially it is impossible to overestimate the importance of "system" play. Practice one style of shot over and over again, with the definite object of making the balls go to certain spots. *The mere having of definite objective points will wonderfully improve your execution.*

I cannot urge too strenuously that the amateur keep firmly in mind the determination not to attempt long drives of both balls, to keep going to the end rails, and of saving the inches. The points of the "do" and "don't" list arising most frequently are these:

When both balls, in balk-line, are "in" get one near the line *on the first shot.*

Avoid shots that leave the balls too closely in the corner.

In close work near the line avoid putting both balls "in" at once. Leave one out.

At first it will be conscious mental effort to keep thinking of these things, but after a time it will become second nature.

What Prevents Players Improving.— Right here let

me say that I do not know of anything that prevents improvement, that keeps fairly good players back in their game so much as making the wrong shot *and then having it come out well.*

To illustrate: You have a certain leave. From one ball you'll gather near the corner lines. From the other farther up toward center table. Suppose you choose the latter, make it perfectly and have the balls all together, *but out in the open table.*

Now up to this point the test of the good or bad judgment of the shot *is still to come.* It comes *when the balls begin to get separated,* and you have to drive. That may be several shots later, and you forget about that first badly chosen shot.

Near the end rail you would have more ways of turning around. In mid-table you generally have only one recovery shot, and that is likely to be a difficult one. If you had taken the right shot in the first place, at the beginning of the run, you would not now be confronted by this dangerous position.

But *here is where the careless player who will not see the point keeps wrong.* Suppose he gets out of this hole, and gets to the ends and goes on. He refuses to see the danger that he was in. He will not realize that in a majority of cases *he would not have gotten out of it.* And the very next time he will repeat that original error and go on doing it, never improving his game.

The Law of Averages in the Choice of Shots.— In life insurance it is an old saying that nothing is so uncertain as the life of a single person, and nothing is so certain as the average life of a large number of persons.

And so it is in billiards. Any one poorly chosen shot may come out well enough, but *it is as certain as fate that the average result* of constant repetition of this same shot will be bad, and that the average result of a large number of well chosen shots will be better.

Now that's what wins in billiards. That's what makes one man a good player, who is improving all the while, the other staying in a rut. And this even though on the individual shot the man in the rut may even be the more skillful in execution.

With one you never know just how well he will play. With the other you never know just how badly he will play. Luck is with one, it is always against the other. So stick to your system.

Don't let the fortunate outcome of a badly chosen shot fool you into thinking that it was *good* billiards instead of *lucky* billiards.

Frank Ives attributed his success to the resolve made early in his career that he would play the "right shot" as a matter of strict system, and if he could not play the shot he would master it.

Say you are in the middle of a run, balls acting kindly. Suddenly they become perverse and you miss a hard one. *How did it happen that you had the hard one to play?* It is generally true that the shot that led to all the trouble, the breaking up of your control, was a poorly chosen or poorly executed one, *two, three or more points back.* The play in whist that determines who gets the "odd" trick is generally one of the early cards, not the late ones. And in billiards it's the same.

Analyze Your Game.— Get in the habit of analyzing

your own game so as to recognize that guilty shot, and steel your mind against repeating it. The habit of self-analysis alone will improve your game.

Cushion Caroms as Practice.— When I advise cushion caroms as part of a program of practice for competitive play I do not mean three-cushion caroms. In the latter game you use the draw shot very little, and the draw is the most important single shot in ball-to-ball billiards. You do not use the one-cushion carom, and that is the most valuable gathering shot in all cushion work.

In real cushion caroms you play position all the time and you get invaluable practice in open table play. Every balk-line player faces the need of skill in this class of shots, and failure in it ends his run. It is well enough in theory to " avoid the need of making hard shots," but it can never be done entirely.

Most runs are stopped by missing open table shots. And every long run must have some of these to make.

Preparing for Contests.— When preparing for a contest play cushion caroms, say, for a week steadily. Then play balk-line up to within a few days of the match. Then drop practice work and play pure, hard contest billiards, playing seriously and playing to win. The earlier practice work will tell its story.

In the *actual contest* make the count first, the position second. Keep the other fellow in his chair.

In practice play go for the position shot as perfectly as possible, neglecting the chance of not counting. In match play make the count sure, the position in its perfection. Let the subconscious effect of your practice take care of that.

On the day of the match it is better to leave the balls alone. A half hour before it make a few practice shots just to limber up and "get the feel" of things, especially draw and nursing shots. But do not keep at it for more than ten or fifteen minutes.

Never change your system in or immediately preceding a match.

On Safety Play.— As a general thing don't be a "safety" player. Speed wins, not safety play. A couple of good runs and you may have the contest all your way, "on ice," as we say. Of course, if one shot is as good as the other, choose the one that will leave them safe if you miss. Or if your opponent has only a few to go, and you a good number, you must take every means to keep him from scoring. But during the major part of the contest safety play is poor tactics.

As to the Stroke.— Cultivate a smooth, even stroke, with decision in it, not timidity, flowing, not jerky — a "measured stroke," as Thomas Gallagher calls it. Concentrate mentally on hitting where you aim, and not on looking at the second object ball.

In a good stroke you do not feel your muscles at work. They do not "gripe" or tighten up. They have none of that contracted feeling, followed by a jerky, explosive effort. It is smoothly flowing, "crescendo"— that is, increasing in decision toward the end, instead of having any feeling of letting up at the end. I have heard it said that every good stroke wants in it at the end just a little "d — n it," just at the instant of contact. There's a good deal in that.

Now a few more practical hints and we are done.

Tips.— See that your cue leather is properly shaped. All good cue men understand this. Personally I do not favor the overlapping leather. I want a foundation back of it. But never have the leather smaller than the cue tip, or the tip will split.

Select a leather neither too hard nor too soft, but favor the latter. It holds the chalk better and does not become glossy so soon.

Miscues are due 90 per cent of the time to faulty aim. It is very difficult to hit a sphere correctly, as the "side" recedes. A little observation will convince you of this. Hit the ball properly and you will gain confidence and make few miscues. Learn to blame your delivery and not the tip.

Always strike the cue ball as near the center as the position sought will permit. Hitting too low for draw shots is likely not only to "jump" the ball, result in a miscue, but may tear the cloth. Hitting too high in a follow shot is likely to make the ball bump and go off at an angle instead of following.

Never "lunge" at a ball in order to strike it hard. Less force and more accuracy will procure better results.

As a rule, let the cue man file or sandpaper your cue. He understands it better.

Educate yourself to the same cue as much as possible. If playing an important match with a short cue, have a long one standing by for long bridge shots.

No good player can execute all he knows all the time. Man is human, not a machine.

Nearly everyone knows, for instance, how a ring is engraved. Only trained muscles can attempt the work, and only a few engravers are "top-notchers." And so in billiards.

No matter how much billiards you know, there is a personal equation, partly of nerves, partly of eyesight, partly of muscular sense and control, as shown in match and tournament play, of that peculiar quality known as "class" that sets limits to one's powers. Some men do their best under pressure and strain, some do their worst.

Knowledge Versus Execution.—Given two players, one strong on execution, a man repeating the same draw or cushion shot fifty times will count forty-five times, the other will count, say, only thirty-five times —the second man, weaker on execution, might easily defeat the other. While he cannot execute so well, he can avoid having to make so many hard shots.

But no matter what the personal equation may be, *knowing more billiards will never make you play worse.*

THE END

A CATALOG OF SELECTED
DOVER BOOKS
IN ALL FIELDS OF INTEREST

A CATALOG OF SELECTED DOVER
BOOKS IN ALL FIELDS OF INTEREST

DRAWINGS OF REMBRANDT, edited by Seymour Slive. Updated Lippmann, Hofstede de Groot edition, with definitive scholarly apparatus. All portraits, biblical sketches, landscapes, nudes. Oriental figures, classical studies, together with selection of work by followers. 550 illustrations. Total of 630pp. 9⅛ × 12¼.
21485-0, 21486-9 Pa., Two-vol. set $29.90

GHOST AND HORROR STORIES OF AMBROSE BIERCE, Ambrose Bierce. 24 tales vividly imagined, strangely prophetic, and decades ahead of their time in technical skill: "The Damned Thing," "An Inhabitant of Carcosa," "The Eyes of the Panther," "Moxon's Master," and 20 more. 199pp. 5⅜ × 8½. 20767-6 Pa. $4.95

ETHICAL WRITINGS OF MAIMONIDES, Maimonides. Most significant ethical works of great medieval sage, newly translated for utmost precision, readability. Laws Concerning Character Traits, Eight Chapters, more. 192pp. 5⅜ × 8½.
24522-5 Pa. $4.50

THE EXPLORATION OF THE COLORADO RIVER AND ITS CANYONS, J. W. Powell. Full text of Powell's 1,000-mile expedition down the fabled Colorado in 1869. Superb account of terrain, geology, vegetation, Indians, famine, mutiny, treacherous rapids, mighty canyons, during exploration of last unknown part of continental U.S. 400pp. 5⅜ × 8½. 20094-9 Pa. $7.95

HISTORY OF PHILOSOPHY, Julián Marías. Clearest one-volume history on the market. Every major philosopher and dozens of others, to Existentialism and later. 505pp. 5⅜ × 8½. 21739-6 Pa. $9.95

ALL ABOUT LIGHTNING, Martin A. Uman. Highly readable non-technical survey of nature and causes of lightning, thunderstorms, ball lightning, St. Elmo's Fire, much more. Illustrated. 192pp. 5⅜ × 8½. 25237-X Pa. $5.95

SAILING ALONE AROUND THE WORLD, Captain Joshua Slocum. First man to sail around the world, alone, in small boat. One of great feats of seamanship told in delightful manner. 67 illustrations. 294pp. 5⅜ × 8½. 20326-3 Pa. $4.95

LETTERS AND NOTES ON THE MANNERS, CUSTOMS AND CONDITIONS OF THE NORTH AMERICAN INDIANS, George Catlin. Classic account of life among Plains Indians: ceremonies, hunt, warfare, etc. 312 plates. 572pp. of text. 6⅛ × 9¼. 22118-0, 22119-9, Pa. Two-vol. set $17.90

ALASKA: The Harriman Expedition, 1899, John Burroughs, John Muir, et al. Informative, engrossing accounts of two-month, 9,000-mile expedition. Native peoples, wildlife, forests, geography, salmon industry, glaciers, more. Profusely illustrated. 240 black-and-white line drawings. 124 black-and-white photographs. 3 maps. Index. 576pp. 5⅜ × 8½. 25109-8 Pa. $11.95

CATALOG OF DOVER BOOKS

ILLUSTRATED DICTIONARY OF HISTORIC ARCHITECTURE, edited by Cyril M. Harris. Extraordinary compendium of clear, concise definitions for over 5,000 important architectural terms complemented by over 2,000 line drawings. Covers full spectrum of architecture from ancient ruins to 20th-century Modernism. Preface. 592pp. 7½ × 9⅜. 24444-X Pa. $15.95

THE NIGHT BEFORE CHRISTMAS, Clement Moore. Full text, and woodcuts from original 1848 book. Also critical, historical material. 19 illustrations. 40pp. 4⅝ × 6. 22797-9 Pa. $2.50

THE LESSON OF JAPANESE ARCHITECTURE: 165 Photographs, Jiro Harada. Memorable gallery of 165 photographs taken in the 1930's of exquisite Japanese homes of the well-to-do and historic buildings. 13 line diagrams. 192pp. 8⅜ × 11¼. 24778-3 Pa. $10.95

THE AUTOBIOGRAPHY OF CHARLES DARWIN AND SELECTED LETTERS, edited by Francis Darwin. The fascinating life of eccentric genius composed of an intimate memoir by Darwin (intended for his children); commentary by his son, Francis; hundreds of fragments from notebooks, journals, papers; and letters to and from Lyell, Hooker, Huxley, Wallace and Henslow. xi + 365pp. 5⅜ × 8. 20479-0 Pa. $6.95

WONDERS OF THE SKY: Observing Rainbows, Comets, Eclipses, the Stars and Other Phenomena, Fred Schaaf. Charming, easy-to-read poetic guide to all manner of celestial events visible to the naked eye. Mock suns, glories, Belt of Venus, more. Illustrated. 299pp. 5¼ × 8¼. 24402-4 Pa. $7.95

BURNHAM'S CELESTIAL HANDBOOK, Robert Burnham, Jr. Thorough guide to the stars beyond our solar system. Exhaustive treatment. Alphabetical by constellation: Andromeda to Cetus in Vol. 1; Chamaeleon to Orion in Vol. 2; and Pavo to Vulpecula in Vol. 3. Hundreds of illustrations. Index in Vol. 3. 2,000pp. 6⅛ × 9¼. 23567-X, 23568-8, 23673-0 Pa., Three-vol. set $41.85

STAR NAMES: Their Lore and Meaning, Richard Hinckley Allen. Fascinating history of names various cultures have given to constellations and literary and folkloristic uses that have been made of stars. Indexes to subjects. Arabic and Greek names. Biblical references. Bibliography. 563pp. 5⅜ × 8½. 21079-0 Pa. $8.95

THIRTY YEARS THAT SHOOK PHYSICS: The Story of Quantum Theory, George Gamow. Lucid, accessible introduction to influential theory of energy and matter. Careful explanations of Dirac's anti-particles, Bohr's model of the atom, much more. 12 plates. Numerous drawings. 240pp. 5⅜ × 8½. 24895-X Pa. $5.95

CHINESE DOMESTIC FURNITURE IN PHOTOGRAPHS AND MEASURED DRAWINGS, Gustav Ecke. A rare volume, now affordably priced for antique collectors, furniture buffs and art historians. Detailed review of styles ranging from early Shang to late Ming. Unabridged republication. 161 black-and-white drawings, photos. Total of 224pp. 8⅜ × 11¼. (Available in U.S. only) 25171-3 Pa. $13.95

VINCENT VAN GOGH: A Biography, Julius Meier-Graefe. Dynamic, penetrating study of artist's life, relationship with brother, Theo, painting techniques, travels, more. Readable, engrossing. 160pp. 5⅜ × 8½. (Available in U.S. only) 25253-1 Pa. $4.95

ILLUSTRATED GUIDE TO SHAKER FURNITURE, Robert Meader. All furniture and appurtenances, with much on unknown local styles. 235 photos. 146pp. 9 × 12. 22819-3 Pa. $8.95

WHALE SHIPS AND WHALING: A Pictorial Survey, George Francis Dow. Over 200 vintage engravings, drawings, photographs of barks, brigs, cutters, other vessels. Also harpoons, lances, whaling guns, many other artifacts. Comprehensive text by foremost authority. 207 black-and-white illustrations. 288pp. 6 × 9. 24808-9 Pa. $9.95

THE BERTRAMS, Anthony Trollope. Powerful portrayal of blind self-will and thwarted ambition includes one of Trollope's most heartrending love stories. 497pp. 5⅜ × 8½. 25119-5 Pa. $9.95

ADVENTURES WITH A HAND LENS, Richard Headstrom. Clearly written guide to observing and studying flowers and grasses, fish scales, moth and insect wings, egg cases, buds, feathers, seeds, leaf scars, moss, molds, ferns, common crystals, etc.—all with an ordinary, inexpensive magnifying glass. 209 exact line drawings aid in your discoveries. 220pp. 5⅜ × 8½. 23330-8 Pa. $4.95

RODIN ON ART AND ARTISTS, Auguste Rodin. Great sculptor's candid, wide-ranging comments on meaning of art; great artists; relation of sculpture to poetry, painting, music; philosophy of life, more. 76 superb black-and-white illustrations of Rodin's sculpture, drawings and prints. 119pp. 8⅜ × 11¼. 24487-3 Pa. $7.95

FIFTY CLASSIC FRENCH FILMS, 1912–1982: A Pictorial Record, Anthony Slide. Memorable stills from Grand Illusion, Beauty and the Beast, Hiroshima, Mon Amour, many more. Credits, plot synopses, reviews, etc. 160pp. 8¼ × 11. 25256-6 Pa. $11.95

THE PRINCIPLES OF PSYCHOLOGY, William James. Famous long course complete, unabridged. Stream of thought, time perception, memory, experimental methods; great work decades ahead of its time. 94 figures. 1,391pp. 5⅜ × 8½. 20381-6, 20382-4 Pa., Two-vol. set $19.90

BODIES IN A BOOKSHOP, R. T. Campbell. Challenging mystery of blackmail and murder with ingenious plot and superbly drawn characters. In the best tradition of British suspense fiction. 192pp. 5⅜ × 8½. 24720-1 Pa. $4.95

CALLAS: PORTRAIT OF A PRIMA DONNA, George Jellinek. Renowned commentator on the musical scene chronicles incredible career and life of the most controversial, fascinating, influential operatic personality of our time. 64 black-and-white photographs. 416pp. 5⅜ × 8¼. 25047-4 Pa. $8.95

GEOMETRY, RELATIVITY AND THE FOURTH DIMENSION, Rudolph Rucker. Exposition of fourth dimension, concepts of relativity as Flatland characters continue adventures. Popular, easily followed yet accurate, profound. 141 illustrations. 133pp. 5⅜ × 8½. 23400-2 Pa. $4.95

HOUSEHOLD STORIES BY THE BROTHERS GRIMM, with pictures by Walter Crane. 53 classic stories—Rumpelstiltskin, Rapunzel, Hansel and Gretel, the Fisherman and his Wife, Snow White, Tom Thumb, Sleeping Beauty, Cinderella, and so much more—lavishly illustrated with original 19th century drawings. 114 illustrations. x + 269pp. 5⅜ × 8½. 21080-4 Pa. $4.95

THE BLUE FAIRY BOOK, Andrew Lang. The first, most famous collection, with many familiar tales: Little Red Riding Hood, Aladdin and the Wonderful Lamp, Puss in Boots, Sleeping Beauty, Hansel and Gretel, Rumpelstiltskin; 37 in all. 138 illustrations. 390pp. 5⅜ × 8½. 21437-0 Pa. $6.95

THE STORY OF THE CHAMPIONS OF THE ROUND TABLE, Howard Pyle. Sir Launcelot, Sir Tristram and Sir Percival in spirited adventures of love and triumph retold in Pyle's inimitable style. 50 drawings, 31 full-page. xviii + 329pp. 6½ × 9¼. 21883-X Pa. $7.95

THE MYTHS OF THE NORTH AMERICAN INDIANS, Lewis Spence. Myths and legends of the Algonquins, Iroquois, Pawnees and Sioux with comprehensive historical and ethnological commentary. 36 illustrations. 5⅜ × 8½.
25967-6 Pa. $8.95

GREAT DINOSAUR HUNTERS AND THEIR DISCOVERIES, Edwin H. Colbert. Fascinating, lavishly illustrated chronicle of dinosaur research, 1820's to 1960. Achievements of Cope, Marsh, Brown, Buckland, Mantell, Huxley, many others. 384pp. 5¼ × 8¼. 24701-5 Pa. $7.95

THE TASTEMAKERS, Russell Lynes. Informal, illustrated social history of American taste 1850's–1950's. First popularized categories Highbrow, Lowbrow, Middlebrow. 129 illustrations. New (1979) afterword. 384pp. 6 × 9.
23993-4 Pa. $8.95

DOUBLE CROSS PURPOSES, Ronald A. Knox. A treasure hunt in the Scottish Highlands, an old map, unidentified corpse, surprise discoveries keep reader guessing in this cleverly intricate tale of financial skullduggery. 2 black-and-white maps. 320pp. 5⅜ × 8½. (Available in U.S. only) 25032-6 Pa. $6.95

AUTHENTIC VICTORIAN DECORATION AND ORNAMENTATION IN FULL COLOR: 46 Plates from "Studies in Design," Christopher Dresser. Superb full-color lithographs reproduced from rare original portfolio of a major Victorian designer. 48pp. 9¼ × 12¼. 25083-0 Pa. $7.95

PRIMITIVE ART, Franz Boas. Remains the best text ever prepared on subject, thoroughly discussing Indian, African, Asian, Australian, and, especially, Northern American primitive art. Over 950 illustrations show ceramics, masks, totem poles, weapons, textiles, paintings, much more. 376pp. 5⅜ × 8. 20025-6 Pa. $7.95

SIDELIGHTS ON RELATIVITY, Albert Einstein. Unabridged republication of two lectures delivered by the great physicist in 1920–21. *Ether and Relativity* and *Geometry and Experience*. Elegant ideas in non-mathematical form, accessible to intelligent layman. vi + 56pp. 5⅜ × 8½. 24511-X Pa. $2.95

THE WIT AND HUMOR OF OSCAR WILDE, edited by Alvin Redman. More than 1,000 ripostes, paradoxes, wisecracks: Work is the curse of the drinking classes, I can resist everything except temptation, etc. 258pp. 5⅜ × 8½. 20602-5 Pa. $4.95

ADVENTURES WITH A MICROSCOPE, Richard Headstrom. 59 adventures with clothing fibers, protozoa, ferns and lichens, roots and leaves, much more. 142 illustrations. 232pp. 5⅜ × 8½. 23471-1 Pa. $3.95

PLANTS OF THE BIBLE, Harold N. Moldenke and Alma L. Moldenke. Standard reference to all 230 plants mentioned in Scriptures. Latin name, biblical reference, uses, modern identity, much more. Unsurpassed encyclopedic resource for scholars, botanists, nature lovers, students of Bible. Bibliography. Indexes. 123 black-and-white illustrations. 384pp. 6 × 9. 25069-5 Pa. $8.95

FAMOUS AMERICAN WOMEN: A Biographical Dictionary from Colonial Times to the Present, Robert McHenry, ed. From Pocahontas to Rosa Parks, 1,035 distinguished American women documented in separate biographical entries. Accurate, up-to-date data, numerous categories, spans 400 years. Indices. 493pp. 6½ × 9¼. 24523-3 Pa. $10.95

THE FABULOUS INTERIORS OF THE GREAT OCEAN LINERS IN HISTORIC PHOTOGRAPHS, William H. Miller, Jr. Some 200 superb photographs capture exquisite interiors of world's great "floating palaces"—1890's to 1980's: *Titanic, Ile de France, Queen Elizabeth, United States, Europa,* more. Approx. 200 black-and-white photographs. Captions. Text. Introduction. 160pp. 8⅞ × 11¾. 24756-2 Pa. $9.95

THE GREAT LUXURY LINERS, 1927–1954: A Photographic Record, William H. Miller, Jr. Nostalgic tribute to heyday of ocean liners. 186 photos of Ile de France, Normandie, Leviathan, Queen Elizabeth, United States, many others. Interior and exterior views. Introduction. Captions. 160pp. 9 × 12. 24056-8 Pa. $10.95

A NATURAL HISTORY OF THE DUCKS, John Charles Phillips. Great landmark of ornithology offers complete detailed coverage of nearly 200 species and subspecies of ducks: gadwall, sheldrake, merganser, pintail, many more. 74 full-color plates, 102 black-and-white. Bibliography. Total of 1,920pp. 8⅜ × 11¼. 25141-1, 25142-X Cloth. Two-vol. set $100.00

THE SEAWEED HANDBOOK: An Illustrated Guide to Seaweeds from North Carolina to Canada, Thomas F. Lee. Concise reference covers 78 species. Scientific and common names, habitat, distribution, more. Finding keys for easy identification. 224pp. 5⅜ × 8½. 25215-9 Pa. $6.95

THE TEN BOOKS OF ARCHITECTURE: The 1755 Leoni Edition, Leon Battista Alberti. Rare classic helped introduce the glories of ancient architecture to the Renaissance. 68 black-and-white plates. 336pp. 8⅜ × 11¼. 25239-6 Pa. $14.95

MISS MACKENZIE, Anthony Trollope. Minor masterpieces by Victorian master unmasks many truths about life in 19th-century England. First inexpensive edition in years. 392pp. 5⅜ × 8½. 25201-9 Pa. $8.95

THE RIME OF THE ANCIENT MARINER, Gustave Doré, Samuel Taylor Coleridge. Dramatic engravings considered by many to be his greatest work. The terrifying space of the open sea, the storms and whirlpools of an unknown ocean, the ice of Antarctica, more—all rendered in a powerful, chilling manner. Full text. 38 plates. 77pp. 9¼ × 12. 22305-1 Pa. $4.95

THE EXPEDITIONS OF ZEBULON MONTGOMERY PIKE, Zebulon Montgomery Pike. Fascinating first-hand accounts (1805–6) of exploration of Mississippi River, Indian wars, capture by Spanish dragoons, much more. 1,088pp. 5⅜ × 8½. 25254-X, 25255-8 Pa. Two-vol. set $25.90

DEGAS: An Intimate Portrait, Ambroise Vollard. Charming, anecdotal memoir by famous art dealer of one of the greatest 19th-century French painters. 14 black-and-white illustrations. Introduction by Harold L. Van Doren. 96pp. 5⅜ × 8½.
25131-4 Pa. $4.95

PERSONAL NARRATIVE OF A PILGRIMAGE TO ALMANDINAH AND MECCAH, Richard Burton. Great travel classic by remarkably colorful personality. Burton, disguised as a Moroccan, visited sacred shrines of Islam, narrowly escaping death. 47 illustrations. 959pp. 5⅜ × 8½. 21217-3, 21218-1 Pa., Two-vol. set $19.90

PHRASE AND WORD ORIGINS, A. H. Holt. Entertaining, reliable, modern study of more than 1,200 colorful words, phrases, origins and histories. Much unexpected information. 254pp. 5⅜ × 8½. 20758-7 Pa. $5.95

THE RED THUMB MARK, R. Austin Freeman. In this first Dr. Thorndyke case, the great scientific detective draws fascinating conclusions from the nature of a single fingerprint. Exciting story, authentic science. 320pp. 5⅜ × 8½. (Available in U.S. only) 25210-8 Pa. $6.95

AN EGYPTIAN HIEROGLYPHIC DICTIONARY, E. A. Wallis Budge. Monumental work containing about 25,000 words or terms that occur in texts ranging from 3000 B.C. to 600 A.D. Each entry consists of a transliteration of the word, the word in hieroglyphs, and the meaning in English. 1,314pp. 6⅜ × 10.
23615-3, 23616-1 Pa., Two-vol. set $35.90

THE COMPLEAT STRATEGYST: Being a Primer on the Theory of Games of Strategy, J. D. Williams. Highly entertaining classic describes, with many illustrated examples, how to select best strategies in conflict situations. Prefaces. Appendices. xvi + 268pp. 5⅜ × 8½. 25101-2 Pa. $6.95

THE ROAD TO OZ, L. Frank Baum. Dorothy meets the Shaggy Man, little Button-Bright and the Rainbow's beautiful daughter in this delightful trip to the magical Land of Oz. 272pp. 5⅜ × 8. 25208-6 Pa. $5.95

POINT AND LINE TO PLANE, Wassily Kandinsky. Seminal exposition of role of point, line, other elements in non-objective painting. Essential to understanding 20th-century art. 127 illustrations. 192pp. 6½ × 9¼. 23808-3 Pa. $5.95

LADY ANNA, Anthony Trollope. Moving chronicle of Countess Lovel's bitter struggle to win for herself and daughter Anna their rightful rank and fortune—perhaps at cost of sanity itself. 384pp. 5⅜ × 8½. 24669-8 Pa. $8.95

EGYPTIAN MAGIC, E. A. Wallis Budge. Sums up all that is known about magic in Ancient Egypt: the role of magic in controlling the gods, powerful amulets that warded off evil spirits, scarabs of immortality, use of wax images, formulas and spells, the secret name, much more. 253pp. 5⅜ × 8½. 22681-6 Pa. $4.50

THE DANCE OF SIVA, Ananda Coomaraswamy. Preeminent authority unfolds the vast metaphysic of India: the revelation of her art, conception of the universe, social organization, etc. 27 reproductions of art masterpieces. 192pp. 5⅜ × 8½.
24817-8 Pa. $5.95

CATALOG OF DOVER BOOKS

THE ART NOUVEAU STYLE BOOK OF ALPHONSE MUCHA: All 72 Plates from "Documents Decoratifs" in Original Color, Alphonse Mucha. Rare copyright-free design portfolio by high priest of Art Nouveau. Jewelry, wallpaper, stained glass, furniture, figure studies, plant and animal motifs, etc. Only complete one-volume edition. 80pp. 9⅜ × 12¼. 24044-4 Pa. $9.95

ANIMALS: 1,419 COPYRIGHT-FREE ILLUSTRATIONS OF MAMMALS, BIRDS, FISH, INSECTS, ETC., edited by Jim Harter. Clear wood engravings present, in extremely lifelike poses, over 1,000 species of animals. One of the most extensive pictorial sourcebooks of its kind. Captions. Index. 284pp. 9 × 12. 23766-4 Pa. $9.95

OBELISTS FLY HIGH, C. Daly King. Masterpiece of American detective fiction, long out of print, involves murder on a 1935 transcontinental flight—"a very thrilling story"—NY Times. Unabridged and unaltered republication of the edition published by William Collins Sons & Co. Ltd., London, 1935. 288pp. 5⅜ × 8½. (Available in U.S. only) 25036-9 Pa. $5.95

VICTORIAN AND EDWARDIAN FASHION: A Photographic Survey, Alison Gernsheim. First fashion history completely illustrated by contemporary photographs. Full text plus 235 photos, 1840-1914, in which many celebrities appear. 240pp. 6½ × 9¼. 24205-6 Pa. $8.95

THE ART OF THE FRENCH ILLUSTRATED BOOK, 1700-1914, Gordon N. Ray. Over 630 superb book illustrations by Fragonard, Delacroix, Daumier, Doré, Grandville, Manet, Mucha, Steinlen, Toulouse-Lautrec and many others. Preface. Introduction. 633 halftones. Indices of artists, authors & titles, binders and provenances. Appendices. Bibliography. 608pp. 8⅜ × 11¼. 25086-5 Pa. $24.95

THE WONDERFUL WIZARD OF OZ, L. Frank Baum. Facsimile in full color of America's finest children's classic. 143 illustrations by W. W. Denslow. 267pp. 5⅜ × 8½. 20691-2 Pa. $7.95

FOLLOWING THE EQUATOR: A Journey Around the World, Mark Twain. Great writer's 1897 account of circumnavigating the globe by steamship. Ironic humor, keen observations, vivid and fascinating descriptions of exotic places. 197 illustrations. 720pp. 5⅜ × 8½. 26113-1 Pa. $15.95

THE FRIENDLY STARS, Martha Evans Martin & Donald Howard Menzel. Classic text marshalls the stars together in an engaging, non-technical survey, presenting them as sources of beauty in night sky. 23 illustrations. Foreword. 2 star charts. Index. 147pp. 5⅜ × 8½. 21099-5 Pa. $3.95

FADS AND FALLACIES IN THE NAME OF SCIENCE, Martin Gardner. Fair, witty appraisal of cranks, quacks, and quackeries of science and pseudoscience: hollow earth, Velikovsky, orgone energy, Dianetics, flying saucers, Bridey Murphy, food and medical fads, etc. Revised, expanded In the Name of Science. "A very able and even-tempered presentation."—The New Yorker. 363pp. 5⅜ × 8. 20394-8 Pa. $6.95

ANCIENT EGYPT: ITS CULTURE AND HISTORY, J. E Manchip White. From pre-dynastics through Ptolemies: society, history, political structure, religion, daily life, literature, cultural heritage. 48 plates. 217pp. 5⅜ × 8½. 22548-8 Pa. $5.95

AMERICAN CLIPPER SHIPS: 1833–1858, Octavius T. Howe & Frederick C. Matthews. Fully-illustrated, encyclopedic review of 352 clipper ships from the period of America's greatest maritime supremacy. Introduction. 109 halftones. 5 black-and-white line illustrations. Index. Total of 928pp. 5⅜ × 8½.
25115-2, 25116-0 Pa., Two-vol. set $17.90

TOWARDS A NEW ARCHITECTURE, Le Corbusier. Pioneering manifesto by great architect, near legendary founder of "International School." Technical and aesthetic theories, views on industry, economics, relation of form to function, "mass-production spirit," much more. Profusely illustrated. Unabridged translation of 13th French edition. Introduction by Frederick Etchells. 320pp. 6⅛ × 9¼. (Available in U.S. only)
25023-7 Pa. $8.95

THE BOOK OF KELLS, edited by Blanche Cirker. Inexpensive collection of 32 full-color, full-page plates from the greatest illuminated manuscript of the Middle Ages, painstakingly reproduced from rare facsimile edition. Publisher's Note. Captions. 32pp. 9⅜ × 12¼.
24345-1 Pa. $4.95

BEST SCIENCE FICTION STORIES OF H. G. WELLS, H. G. Wells. Full novel *The Invisible Man*, plus 17 short stories: "The Crystal Egg," "Aepyornis Island," "The Strange Orchid," etc. 303pp. 5⅜ × 8½. (Available in U.S. only)
21531-8 Pa. $6.95

AMERICAN SAILING SHIPS: Their Plans and History, Charles G. Davis. Photos, construction details of schooners, frigates, clippers, other sailcraft of 18th to early 20th centuries—plus entertaining discourse on design, rigging, nau' ' lore, much more. 137 black-and-white illustrations. 240pp. 6⅛ × 9¼.
24658-2 Pa. $6.95

ENTERTAINING MATHEMATICAL PUZZLES, Martin Gardner. Selection of author's favorite conundrums involving arithmetic, money, speed, etc., with lively commentary. Complete solutions. 112pp. 5⅜ × 8½.
25211-6 Pa. $2.95

THE WILL TO BELIEVE, HUMAN IMMORTALITY, William James. Two books bound together. Effect of irrational on logical, and arguments for human immortality. 402pp. 5⅜ × 8½.
20291-7 Pa. $7.95

THE HAUNTED MONASTERY and THE CHINESE MAZE MURDERS, Robert Van Gulik. 2 full novels by Van Gulik continue adventures of Judge Dee and his companions. An evil Taoist monastery, seemingly supernatural events; overgrown topiary maze that hides strange crimes. Set in 7th-century China. 27 illustrations. 328pp. 5⅜ × 8½.
23502-5 Pa. $6.95

CELEBRATED CASES OF JUDGE DEE (DEE GOONG AN), translated by Robert Van Gulik. Authentic 18th-century Chinese detective novel; Dee and associates solve three interlocked cases. Led to Van Gulik's own stories with same characters. Extensive introduction. 9 illustrations. 237pp. 5⅜ × 8½.
23337-5 Pa. $5.95

Prices subject to change without notice.

Available at your book dealer or write for free catalog to Dept. GI, Dover Publications, Inc., 31 East 2nd St., Mineola, N.Y. 11501. Dover publishes more than 175 books each year on science, elementary and advanced mathematics, biology, music, art, literary history, social sciences and other areas.